Garrett Davis

Speech of Hon. Garrett Davis of Kentucky on the state of the Union

Union

1864

Garrett Davis

Speech of Hon. Garrett Davis of Kentucky on the state of the Union
1864

ISBN/EAN: 9783337175894

Printed in Europe, USA, Canada, Australia, Japan

Cover: Foto ©Suzi / pixelio.de

More available books at **www.hansebooks.com**

SPEECH

OF

HON. GARRETT DAVIS,

OF KENTUCKY,

ON

THE STATE OF THE UNION;

IN

WHICH HE GAVE A SKETCH OF THE POLITICAL HISTORY OF MASSACHUSETTS.

DELIVERED

IN THE SENATE OF THE UNITED STATES,

FEBRUARY 16 & 17, 1864.

———————

WASHINGTON:
L. TOWERS & CO., PRINTERS.
1864.

SPEECH

OF

HON. GARRETT DAVIS, OF KY.,

ON

THE STATE OF THE UNION;

IN WHICH HE GAVE A SKETCH OF THE POLITICAL HISTORY OF MASSACHUSETTS.

DELIVERED IN THE SENATE OF THE UNITED STATES, FEBRUARY 16 & 17, 1864.

The Senate having under consideration the bill to equalize the pay of soldiers, Mr. DAVIS said:

Mr. PRESIDENT: A great man once asked the question what a public man was worth who would not stand or fall by a great principle. I expand that question, and I ask, what is any man worth who will not stand or fall by a great principle? Sir, I have that amount of value at least. Some gentlemen on this floor in the course of former debates have said truly that I was fond of recurring to the past. When I make a retrospect of the past, even for only a few years, how great and melancholy is the contrast with the present! Then we had peace, fraternity, unity, prosperity, power, and the respect of the nations of the world. That retrospect gives me a mournful pleasure. I love to dwell upon those halcyon times, times which I sincerely apprehend have left this country to return no more, at least so long as myself, a much older man than you, and you, sir, [Mr. HOWE in the chair,] shall be living.

Mr. President, I have seen somewhere faction defined to be "the madness of the many for the benefit of the few." Parties are inherent, and indeed inevitable, in all popular Governments, and generally arise in all Governments. When parties are formed on diverse opinions of principles and measures of policy, and their effects upon the Government and the country, and the differences of their probable effects are investigated and maintained with truth and candor, they are useful in forming a correct public opinion, in repressing maladministration, and in upholding liberty and the true spirit of the Government. But when these parties turn away from truth and reason, disregard fundamental principles, and support men not because of their fitness for office, their virtues, intelligence, and fidelity to public trusts and duty; and measures not because they are wise and just and promotive of the public good, but because they promise to subserve the ends, the ambition, and passions of individuals, or to attain or hold power, party then becomes faction.

In the first and purer days of most free Governments the people generally divide into *parties*, but the selfishness and arts of the leaders and the credulity of the masses soon cause them to degenerate into factions. Country then becomes absorbed by party, truth and reason by falsehood and passion, and the public good and glory by partisan contests and triumphs. Then there is enacted the "madness of the many for the benefit of the few." The masses surrender their judgment, their will, and their conduct to their leaders, and become their followers and slaves, and ignore wholly the merits of men and measures. Party fealty, the *esprit de corps* of party, becomes the strongest bond among men, dominates their opinions, lives, and acts, and directs the destiny of the nation. Each succeeding faction becomes more venal, corrupt, and desperate than its predecessor, their conflicts becomes fiercer, the ligaments of society are loosened, law and order are disregarded, private pursuits and industry are disturbed, property is seized upon by rapacious armed men, liberty and life become unsafe, and the people, growing weary and disgusted with the ever-recurring and never-ending turmoil, for a modicum of tranquillity and security at length accept a despotism and a master. The positions here stated are all proved

4

by the successive factions in ancient Rome, of Marius, of Sylla, of Pompey, Julius Cæsar and Crassus, of Antony, Lepidus, and Octavius, and the natural and inevitable consummation, the establishment of an imperial despotism by Octavius Cæsar. Corroborative examples could be readily adduced from the history of many other countries, ancient and modern, as well as the present deplorable condition of the United States; and the measures, purposes, and spirit of the parties North and South which now rule them, give mournful assurance that they too may add another and incomparably the strongest of the numerous examples which the enemies of free institutions are so fond of citing, to prove that well ordered and permanent self-government is impossible to be achieved by any people.

It seems to me that the decline of the *great Republic* has commenced in its early immaturity, and has progressed and is progressing with a rapidity beyond all precedent. I never indulged the dream that it could be immortal, perpetual; but I clung to the faith that it would have its periods of active youth, of vigorous manhood, and sound old age; and that each period would be measured by centuries. If its destiny should be thus early to fall, it will not only be the most untimely but the noblest ruin that was ever mourned by mankind, blasting, beyond all comparison, for the present and through long-coming ages, more of the world's hope.

I never for a moment doubted that the rebellion would be suppressed, and when the news of the disastrous battle of Bull Run reached my town, and there struck down the spirit of every other Union man, I expressed to them my conviction that that reverse would arouse a spirit which would call out the entire resources of the loyal States; and although they might be more slow in being made available, they were so superior in force and endurance and all material wealth, that the rebels must be overwhelmed, and that consummation was only a question of time. I have held to that opinion without ever having a moment of doubt.

I came to the Senate soon after the President and the two Houses of Congress had with unprecedented unanimity declared to the people of the United States and to the world in the clearest language the principles and ends upon and for which the war against the rebels should be conducted. I put my trust and faith in those declarations and in the men who made them, and while they were observed I not only supported their war measures, but gave them personally my fullest confidence. But a new policy for conducting the war, and essentially different from that previously announced by the President and by Congress, began to be evolved. The President has since fully developed and is now fearfully executing it. When he violated the many and distinct and emphatic pledges upon which and by which he was bound to conduct the war, for one, my confidence in him died to live no more. But what I consider to be the great perfidy of the President has not and never will cause me to hesitate to support the Government and the Union of these States in this civil war. I have voted for every measure to strengthen the executive arm that I deemed to be constitutional, and for some about which, both as to constitutionality and policy, I entertained serious doubts, and this because of the great stress of the country, and the desire of the Executive to have them enacted into laws. I shall continue this course of official conduct, not for the President or the party in power, but for the Constitution which I have sworn to support, for the restoration of the Union of the States, and for the common and permanent welfare of my country.

It is this great civil war and its continuance that has brought the President to enormous abuses and usurpations of power, and the people to submit to them so passively. If the war could be closed speedily, they, too, would soon come to an end; but so long as it continues, the only hope of their reformation is in the election of another President, and here arises a mighty motive with those in power and office, and in the receipt of large emoluments, for its continuance. It seems to me, too, that the rebels will rally all their energies for a decisive struggle in the coming campaign. I do not doubt that their great armies will be routed and driven from the field; the mass, however, will fight to extermination before they will submit to the humiliating terms that have been prescribed for them by the President. The rebel armies, unable to maintain great campaigns, will break up into small bodies, and from their swamps and mountain fastnesses will carry on a desolating partisan war for a longer period than Circassia did against Russia; and before it can be terminated by their subjugation, constitutional government and popular liberty throughout the United States may have perished, not for a time, but forever. I have never feared, nor have I now the least apprehension of the permanent overthrow of free institutions anywhere in the United States, by Jefferson Davis and his government; but I am beset by the gloomiest apprehensions that if Mr. Lincoln is re-elected, or some other man having his principles, policy, and scheme of government should be his successor, they will perish by him and his government, or by stronger men who will rise up and thrust them from their places.

No men ever charged with the possession and administration of a free Government devised so bold and so extensive a scheme for its revolution, or were so prompt and successful in its execution, as the men who hold possession of the Government of the United States. The strong and fixed attachment of the loyal States to the Union; the general aversion of the people of the free States to slavery, and the fanatical and active hostility of a large sectional party to it; the inauguration of the rebellion exclusively by slave States, and the absorbing devotion of large portions of their people to their peculiar institution; the magnitude of the military power and resources which the rebels brought into the field to support their revolt and achieve their independence; the enormous armies, equipments, and supplies which the United States had to organize to meet successfully their formidable enemy; and the fierceness with which the war has been waged on both sides, have given to ambitious men in power such an opportunity as never occurred before in any country to trample down the Constitution, laws, and liberties of the people, and to seize upon indefinite arbitrary power. Backed by a resistless military force ramified all over the loyal States, the assumptions of power by those in authority have been in proportion to the dimensions of the rebellion, and the people, confounded by the great and threatening danger to the Union and the extent and audacity of those usurpations, have given but little heed to their Constitution, rights and liberties, thinking that when the terrific storm had passed they would resume their wonted position, security, and vitality. Fatal delusion! Those inappreciable blessings of Government, once yielded by a people, are generally lost forever; they are never regained except at the cost of countless sufferings and seas of blood. The duty that devolved upon the people in this great exigency required high intelligence, virtue, courage, and fortitude; it was at the same time to put down the rebellion, and to hold all their agents, civil and military, strictly and firmly within the limits of their constitutional and legal powers. Had that great duty been performed and the civil and military affairs of the country been wisely administered the rebellion would ere this have been suppressed, the Union and peace restored, and our institutions strengthened and enshrined anew in the hearts of our country-men and more strongly commended to the acceptance of mankind. The best that can now be done is to occupy as much as possible of that safe anchorage.

Political liberty in England was of Saxon birth. It fell temporarily by the victory of William the Conqueror at Hastings; but the Saxons, who were still much the larger portion of the people, were deeply imbued with its spirit. It soon burst forth vigorously against the tyranny of the feudal system and the Normans, and made brave and unceasing conflict with the Plantagenets for their ancient rights; and the sturdy barons, under the feeble John, achieved their reconquest from the throne. This contest between parliamentary privilege and popular liberty on the one side, and kingly prerogative on the other, was resumed and continued throughout the reigns of the succeeding Plantagenets and all the Tudors. The kings claimed the essential powers of Government, both executive and legislative, as of their prerogative; the Commons of England asserted as of their privilege as the third estate, representing the people, that no laws could be enacted or suspended without their concurrence, and that all the rights, privileges, and liberties founded under their Saxon kings, and restored by Magna Charta, were the birthright of every Englishman, This great contest, extending through centuries, was taken up by Hampden and Cromwell and their heroic associates, and brought to a final issue in favor of the privileges of Parliament and the liberties of the people in the reign of Charles I. They were defined more clearly and established more firmly by various acts of Parliament, passed in the reigns of Charles II, William of Orange, and at the accession of George I; and they have ever since been as firmly moored in the British constitution and Government as the isle itself in its ocean bed.

But in our free and limited Government of a written Constitution, President Lincoln and his party, in utter disregard of its limitations and restrictions, are making for him as President claim to the same boundless and despotic powers, executive and legislative, which the Plantagenets, the Tudors, and the first Stuarts contended for in England as appertaining to the kingly prerogative, through so many generations of convulsive and bloody struggle, and which they ultimately lost, after the longest, truest, most steady and heroic devotion to their rights and liberties by the people of England that is to be found in the history of mankind. Those inestimable rights, liberties, privileges, and institutions, secured forever, it is to be hoped, to that people by their appreciating sense, manly virtues, and insucible fortitude, our ancestors brought with them to this continent; and the founders of our Government thought they had secured them to the people of the United States beyond all changes and chances, by setting them forth as fundamental principles in their written form of Government; and yet the President has seized upon the opportunity of this great rebellion to subvert them for the time, and if he is re-elected to the Presidency that subversion will become complete and final. His overthrow, or that of the Constitution and popular liberty, is inevitable; and it is yet in the power of the American people to decide this great issue in favor of Constitution and liberty, if they will throw off their lethargy and arouse themselves to the most important work that has ever been intrusted to man.

Mr. President, no Government could be organized in this enlightened age without adequate provisions for the protection of private property. It is one of the great ends for which society and all government are formed, and consequently it is one of the prominent objects that was attempted to be secured by the Constitution of the United States. The fifth article of the Amendments expresses the principle of the Constitution upon that point in clear and precise language. I will read it:

"No person shall be held to answer for a capital, or otherwise infamous crime, unless on a presentment or indictment of a grand jury, except in cases arising in the land or naval forces, or in the militia, when in actual service in time of war or public danger; nor shall any person be subject for the same offence to be twice put in jeopardy of life or limb; nor shall be compelled in any criminal case to be a witness against himself, nor be deprived of life, liberty, or property, without due process of law; nor shall private property be taken for public use without just compensation."

Mr. President, some gentlemen assume the most extraordinary and absurd position that negroes are not and cannot be the subject of property. Our Constitution recognizes property in slaves. The courts of the United States, which by the Constitution are expressly empowered to decide all cases arising under that instrument, uniformly and in numerous cases have recognized property in African slaves. There is not a civilized country of the earth, where this question ever arose, whose high judicial tribunals have not sustained the same position. Slavery and property in slaves have been upheld by the laws, usages, and practice of nations of the highest civilization from before the first dawn of history. This question has been made, not only in the Supreme Court of the United States, but also repeatedly in the circuit courts of the United States for Ohio and Michigan, and in one case at least the honorable Senator from Michigan [Mr. Howard] appeared as counsel. The courts sustained, not only the right of property in the owners of slaves, but also that where they were fugitive, and escaped into other States, the owner or his agent could go into that State, and, against its express law to the contrary, seize his slave and take him back; and if he was resisted by any persons to the loss of the slave, or they aided the slave to escape, the owner could sue the persons interfering in the United States courts, and recover from them both the reasonable value of the slave and a penalty for their interference. The man who contends in the United States that African slaves are not and cannot be the subject of property is *non compos mentis*.

In relation to this matter of property in slaves as connected with my own State, how does it stand? We have in Kentucky about, I will say in round numbers, two hundred and fifty thousand negro slaves. Before the commencement of this rebellion they were worth $600 average at least. A colleague of mine in the other House, who is my near neighbor and among the largest owners of slaves in the State, estimates their value according to an appraisement which he has made of some that he placed upon a cotton farm in the South, men, women, and children, at $800 a head; but a moderate and reasonable estimate would be $600 average. Two hundred and fifty thousand slaves at that rate would be worth $150,000,000. That is one-fourth part of the aggregate wealth of the State of Kentucky. What does this measure and the series of cognate measures in relation to the same subject contemplate? To deprive the people of the State of Kentucky of $150,000,000 of their property which is guarantied to them not only by their own constitution and laws, but also by the Constitution of the United States and by all the decisions, both Federal and State, of all the courts in the United States, I believe, with one solitary exception in a State court of Wisconsin, and which has been properly reversed by the revisory judgment of a United States court. Is it not a question of a good deal of magnitude to my constituency whether the President or Congress shall, directly or indirectly, deprive them of that amount of property without any compensation? But, sir, the Congress of the United States, nor the President, have not a particle of jurisdiction or power over the subject to the extent of liberating slaves. Neither has any military officer any more rightful authority to set free a slave in the State of Kentucky than has the levy court of the county of Washington.

Mr. WILKINSON rose.

Mr. DAVIS. I would rather the Senator would reserve his questions until I get through, and then I will answer them with great pleasure; but I prefer not to be interrupted. I say it most courteously to the honorable Senator.

The PRESIDING OFFICER, (Mr. Howe in the chair.) The Senator from Kentucky is entitled to the floor.

Mr. DAVIS. Mr. President, we have a peculiar and unique Government. We have a Government established by a written Constitution. That Constitution is the law of our Government, and limits all its power and authority. It has been decided again and again by the Supreme Court, and it is the plainest dictate of reason and common intelligence, much less of legal learning, that the Government of the United States cannot claim, or exercise without usurpation, a solitary power that is not conferred upon it by that sole law of its creation. The Constitution was formed by separate, distinct, and independent political sovereignties, each one of those sovereignties within its own limits and jurisdiction being clothed with all political power. They saw the necessity of a common national Government, and consequently of a surrender of some of the highest powers of political sovereignty to that national Government for the purpose of securing the welfare of the whole people of the United States. This surrender of power was almost mainly of the character of those that appertain to the foreign relations of the States or their relations with each other. It is one of the essential features of the system that the domestic institutions, laws, and polity of each State were not surrendered to the General Government, but were retained almost wholly and exclusively by the States.

Now, Mr. President, in the face of the guaranties in the Constitution which I have read, that private property shall not be taken except for public use, and by judgment of law and upon compensation being made to the owner, how can the Government of the United States, in any of its departments, seize and appropriate private property for any other object than public use, public appropriation, public application of the property to some purpose and action of Government? And when it takes private property, even for such ends, how can it presume to take that property, in the face of this provision of the Constitution, without making, or intending to make, compensation to the owners for it?

Mr. President, an error is committed very often in this day, and I think it is for the want of a recurrence to and an examination of the essays and explanations of and that were contemporaneous with the Constitution. Gentlemen attempt to analyze, to define, to enlarge the powers of our Government by comparing it with other Governments. As I said before, our Government is unique. It is formed by a written instrument. That instrument speaks for itself. It was formed upon the general principle of not giving plenary powers to the national Government, but only such as should be delegated to it by the States, and not to be obligatory upon any State that did not ratify it. This principle has been often announced by the Supreme Court, that only such powers are vested in the General Government as are expressly delegated by the language of the Constitution itself or by the necessary, reasonable, and proper implication of that language. A leading feature of the Government is that all the powers vested in the President by the Constitution are enumerated in the second and third sections of the second article; and he is not clothed with a solitary incidental power, but the whole of that unnumbered and indefinite class of powers are vested by the express and unequivocal language of the Constitution itself in Congress, and that only to the extent that they are necessary and proper to enable Congress, or the President, or the judiciary, or any other department or officer of the Government to execute the powers with which they are expressly clothed. Congress may assume and exercise itself at pleasure any of those incidental powers, but the President or any other officer not one of them until authorized by a law of Congress. This Government of limited authority is also by express provisions restricted or forbid to exercise sundry enumerated powers; and there is also a direct provision that the express restriction of any powers to the General Government shall have no effect whatever to grant it any additional power or to enlarge those that are vested by the Constitution.

Sir, what is another general principle of our Government? That all the powers of Government established by the language of the Constitution are expressly in the main parted and divided among three departments, and the powers that are to be exercised by each are expressly enumerated. Then when a question arises as to the general proposition of the extent of the powers of the Federal Government, or of their investiture in what department or officer, there is but one rule of construction, and that rule is the language of the Constitution itself, and the condition of the country and public affairs when it was adopted. There is no other system of government under the sun that can enlighten legislators or the President or courts upon such questions. You may resort to the British Government as it then existed, and the writings of publicists when the Constitution was adopted, to ascertain the meaning, import, and force of terms of art or political science that are introduced into the Constitution, but beyond that you cannot have reference to any Government, not for the purpose of illustrating or ascertaining what are the powers of the Government of the United States, or in what departments and magistracies they may be deposited, but on these questions you have to look to the Constitution alone.

Sir, in construing the Holy Scripture you might as well recur to the Koran, to the Puranas of the Hindoos, to the system of Zoroaster, to the moral precepts taught by Confucius or Seneca or any other great heathen moralist, with as much propriety as you may resort to other systems of government to determine and ascertain what are the powers and what are the depositories of the powers of our Government. Our Constitution is our political Bible, and as such is as much distinct and isolated from the constitutions and governments of all other countries as the Christian's Bible is from all other systems of religion.

Then, sir, I come to this other cardinal principle, which I lay down as an incontrovertible axiom, that wherever the Constitution of the United States by express language establishes and vests a power of government, or guaranties a right, liberty, or privilege to the citizen, such provision of the Constitution cannot be suspended or abrogated, restricted or impaired in its operation by any implication arising from any other of the provisions of the Constitution. I also state this further principle as axiomatic: that the amendments to the Constitution being the last expressed will of the people upon the subject of their Government, like amendments to all laws and constitutions, if there be any conflict express or by implication between the original text and the amendments, the amendments are to prevail, and are to give the supreme and the undoubted law upon the controverted point. Then, sir, I recur to the Constitution and read the provision guarantying the rights of private property in the most explicit language—one of the cardinal ends for which this and all other legitimate Government was created, without which express guarantee of property and other inalienable rights and liberties the people of the United States were not satisfied in the first instance with the Constitution; and I assert that there are no other express provisions overruling them, or conflicting to any extent with them: and that they cannot be nullified, restricted, or affected by any possible implications springing out of the other provisions of the Constitution, or out of the whole of it. Sir, that position in truth and in sound logic ends the controversy. When I read these guarantees of private property, and the emphatic declaration that it shall be taken but for public uses, and then only on just compensation being made, there is an end to the question of the right of the citizen to have a fair price for his property where it is taken for public use. The argument cannot be answered.

Now, sir, what does this joint resolution propose to do? It proposes to take slave property without making any compensation to the owners: and here let me examine the question: What is just compensation for private property? Has the Government of the United States, or any of its authorities or officers, civil or military, the right to wrest a man's property from him without he receiving compensation for it at the time, or within a reasonable period thereafter? I answer, no. If a military officer says that he takes it for the public service, and because the exigencies of that service require him to take it, and that is all he says or does or is authorized to do by his Government in relation to making just compensation for property, and there are no means of making compensation by law, I ask does that satisfy in any sense the requisitions of the Constitution?

The constitutions of the different States have similar provisions in relation to taking private property for public use. The constitution of my own State has a provision almost in the same words, and I believe that most of the State constitutions have a similar provision. What have been the adjudications of the supreme court of the State of Kentucky in relation to that provision? The extreme point which they have ruled in relation to the power of the Government in its favor is, that there must be laws in force and effect authorizing the levy of money upon the State for the purpose of making this compensation; and these laws must be executed by the proper court assessing so much money as will be sufficient to pay a fair and reasonable price for the property that is so taken; and they have decided in explicit terms that any state of case or of law short of such a provision as that does not satisfy the requirements of the Constitution. The legal consequence is, that the taking of property, even for public use, under any other state of case, would be a wrong to the owner; and the officer so taking it could be sued and held liable as a trespasser.

Is not that proposition obvious to every man of good sense? Shall the Government any more than an individual, in the exercise, if you please, of its high power of sovereignty, take private property without making or offering to make or having made any provision whatever for its fair value to the owner? Yet such is the practice and the constant practice of our Government. It is in derogation of the Constitution and the rights of property guarantied to the citizen. The question might well arise when the property was taken from the citizen if compensation therefor should not then and there be made. But until there are laws which authorize the valuation of the property and the assessment of money to pay the owner for it, there is not a pretense that the guarantee of the Constitution has been satisfied.

Here is another violation of this principle by the course of the Government in the practices of its military officers. What power has a United States agent, civil or military, to take private property and to place his own value upon it? What right has a recruiting officer, or the Secretary of War, or the President, to enlist a negro man and to assess $300 as his value, if any be assessed, when, if his time and service were assured to his owner or the birer from that owner, he would be worth from two to three hundred dollars a year? What right has the Government of the United States, or any of its agents, to seize any property, whatever, that is necessary for the uses of the Army, or for any other branch of the public service, and arbitrarily to assess their own value upon it? There is but one mode in which that can be properly and legally done; and that is for disinterested commissioners or appraisers to be selected by authority of law, to ascertain the fair and reasonable value of the property, whatever it may be; and for the United States to have a course of proceedings ready provided for by law, and to put them in course of execution, for making to the owner of the property the fair compensation for it at the time that he is deprived of its possession. Sir, a Government that acts upon a different principle is oppressive, is tyrannical; it violates flagrantly the requisitions of the Constitution and the rights of the citizen; it does not answer the purposes and ends for which the people organized their Government. They never intended or formed their Government to wrong and oppress them; and the highest obligation of its officials is to be just to the people.

But, Mr. President, a great deal is claimed in this day of insurrection and civil war under the pretext "military necessity." Sir, I deny that there is any such power as that in our Government that will sanction the enormous abuses of power that have been perpetrated during this war. That question was up before the Supreme Court in the case of Mitchell vs. Harmony—a case that arose during the Mexican war. I will read from 13 Howard's Reports a page or two of the opinion that will give the general facts of the case, and the principles that arose and were decided in it:

"He (the defendant) justified the seizure on several grounds:
"1. That the plaintiff was engaged in trading with the enemy.
"2. That he was compelled to remain with the American forces, and to move with them, to prevent the property from falling into the hands of the enemy.
"3. That the property was taken for public use.
"4. That if the defendant was liable for the original taking he was released from damages for its subsequent loss by the act of the plaintiff, who had resumed the possession and control of it before the loss happened.
"5. That the defendant acted in obedience to the order of his commanding officer, and therefore is not liable.
"The first objection was overruled by the court, and we think correctly."

The opinion then goes on to the second and third objections, which contain the material parts of the opinion, as they bear on the principles decided in the case:

"The second and third objections will be considered together, as they depend on the same principles. Upon these two grounds of defense the circuit court instructed the jury that the defendant might lawfully take possession of the goods of the plaintiff, to prevent them from falling into the hands of the public enemy; but in order to justify the seizure the danger must be immediate and impending, and not remote or contingent. And that he might also take them for public use and impress them into the public service, in case of an immediate and pressing danger or urgent necessity existing at the time, but not otherwise.

"In the argument of these two points, the circumstances under which the goods of the plaintiff were taken have been much discussed, and the evidence examined for the purpose of showing the nature and character of the danger which actually existed at the time or was apprehended by the commander of the American forces. But this question is not before us. It is a question of fact upon which the jury have passed, and their verdict has decided that a danger or necessity such as the court described did not exist when the property of the plaintiff was taken by the defendant. And the only subject for inquiry in this court is, whether the law was correctly stated in the instruction of the court; and whether anything short of an immediate and impending danger from the public enemy or an urgent necessity for the public service can justify the taking of private property by a military commander to prevent it from falling into the hands of the enemy, or for the purpose of converting it to the use of the enemy.

"The instruction is objected to on the ground that it restricts the power of the officer within narrower limits than the law will justify; and that when the troops are employed in an expedition into the enemy's country, where the danger that meets them cannot always be foreseen, and where they are cut off from aid of their own Government, the commanding officer must necessarily be intrusted with some discretionary power as to the measures he should adopt; and if he acts honestly and to the best of his judgment, the law will protect him. But it must be remembered that the question here is not as to the discretion he may exercise in his military operations or in relation to those who are under his command His distance from home, and the duties in which he is engaged, cannot enlarge his power over the property of a citizen, nor give to him in that respect any authority which he would not under similar circumstances possess at home. And where the owner has done nothing to forfeit his rights, every public officer is bound to respect them, whether he finds the property in a foreign or hostile country or in his own.

"There are, without doubt, occasions in which private property may lawfully be taken possession of or destroyed to prevent it from falling into the hands of the public enemy: and also where a military officer, charged with a particular duty, may impress private property into the public service, or take it for public use. Unquestionably, in such cases, the Government is bound to make full compensation to the owner; but the officer is not a trespasser.

"But we are clearly of opinion that in all these cases the danger must be immediate and impending, or the necessity urgent for the public service, such as will not admit of delay, and where the action of the civil authority would be too late in providing the means which the occasion calls for. It is impossible to define the particular circumstances of danger or necessity in which this power may be lawfully exercised. Every case must depend on its own circumstances. It is the emergency that gives the right, and the emergency must be shown to exist before the taking can be justified."

It goes on then further to state that if the commander of the expedition himself, General Doniphan, who gave the order, had been there doing the act of taking possession of the property, he himself would not have been justified but would have been a trespasser, and that the order of a superior to an inferior to do an illegal act still leaves that act, though performed in obedience to positive orders, a trespass, and the subordinate is responsible for it as a trespasser. But the two main principles decided are these: first, private property cannot be seized by a military man unless the danger that creates this necessity be so immediate and impending, the case so urgent, that it cannot wait for the action of the civil authorities; second, where the urgency and necessity is of that character that cannot await, still, if the property is seized, it is in every instance upon the condition that the Government is bound to make reasonable and just compensation for it to the owner.

Now, sir, these are the two principles which this case establishes; and they are as favorable to the Government and its agents as the provisions of the Constitution can authorize any enlightened court to lay down. They go to the very verge that can be claimed by any military commander whatever, even the Commander in-Chief.

But, sir, if that case of urgent, impending necessity that cannot wait the action of the civil authorities be upon an officer, although he may justify himself against an action of trespass, yet in establishing such a case of necessity, it to no extent exempts the United States from their liability to make compensation for the property.

Now, sir, the amendments which I propose to offer, if the joint resolution shall assume a shape to make it in order, contemplate two or three movements upon the part of our Government: first, that so far as negroes free or slave are soldiers they shall be disbanded and disarmed; that as many of them as are necessary in the service of the United States as teamsters or laborers may be so retained by the order of the President, but they are to be retained as private property, and commanders of the regiments to which they are attached in the service are to give a certificate of their employment in the service of the United States, and their owners are to be entitled quarterly to a reasonable compensation for their services.

Sir, it would be the wisest policy that this Government could adopt to accept the first branch of my proposition. Those negroes should never have been enrolled as a part of the Army of the United States. It was a great and a fatal mistake. The best that now can be done is to retrace that erroneous step as rapidly as we can. Sir, this rebellion has been strengthened to an incalculable degree by the employment of negro soldiers. The policy, the system upon which the war has been conducted, has had no other effect than to unite and knit together the southern people firmly, indissolubly almost, and to call forth their utmost force and resources to the support of their rebellion. It has alarmed and deeply dissatisfied the loyal population of the border slave States, been a grievous injustice and oppression to that class of population in the rebel States, and caused everywhere oppressive measures that have produced wide-spread discontent in all the loyal States.

Sir, there was not a power necessary to have enabled the Government to subdue, in a reasonable time, this rebellion, that could not have been properly conferred upon it by constitutional legislation, and that would not have been literally in conformity to the Crittenden resolution and of the President's pledges in relation to the war.

But, sir, if the error, and, in my judgment, the fatal error, in enrolling negro soldiers is not to be retraced, we then come to that impregnable constitutional provision that private property whether a slave or any other class of property, cannot be taken for the use of the Government without making the owner fair, just, and reasonable compensation. If the Senate should be indisposed to accept my first proposition, it ought at least to take the second. If it is resolved to have the military services of the negro, it must, in obedience to all the decisions of the Supreme Court, recognize the negro, where he is a slave, as property, and it must, in obedience to those decisions, as well as to the express provision of the Constitution, make provision for the payment of his fair value to the owner.

Mr. President, I will add one other word in connection with this branch of the subject. There are some gentlemen in this Chamber who were invited with other gentlemen, including myself, from the border slave States, to meet the President in consultation some two years ago in relation to slavery in the border States. On that occasion the President renewed his pledges, in the most explicit and clear language, that it was not his purpose to interfere with slavery in the States. He then admitted, in the most plain and distinct terms, that there were the same constitutional and legal guarantees to the owner of that property as to the owner of any other class of property. As I have stated before once or twice on this floor, he put this pointed case. "I," said the President, "earn $1,000, and I invest that money in land; another individual earns $1,000 and invests it in a negro slave; he has as indefeasable a right to his slave as I have to my land."

He added furthermore, "I am not yet prepared to break with Greely and company." A gentleman from Maryland suggested to him that the rights of the owners of that description of property were already being threatened to be infringed in that State. He then with emotion asseverated, "If I live until the 4th of March, 1865, I will remain President of the United States, and this property shall be protected in Maryland." A gentleman from that State then suggested to the President that the effect and substance of the conference between him and the gentlemen present should be reduced to writing. The President warmed up somewhat, and with some earnestness directed this question to that gentleman, "Do you see any of the snake in me?" I then thought that he had none of the snake in him, but how I have changed my opinion since! He was then dissembling; he has practiced the obliquity and crawling, stealthy movement of the snake towards its object upon the whole of the institution of slavery, though he then made professions so different to the gentlemen who surrounded him.

But, Mr. President, I have some authority here on the subject of property in slaves that I beg leave to lay before the Senate. Both the members from Massachusetts assume audaciously that there is not and cannot be property in negroes because they are human beings. Sir, Massachusetts herself has a history upon this subject, and I will read a little from that history. Let us see how Massachusetts used to think and to act and to trade and to legislate upon the subject of negro slavery and property in slaves. I ask those gentlemen when and where and by whom was negro slavery established in the American colonies—who but by Massachusetts herself? What does her history answer on these points of inquiry? A day of recent celebration of the sodality of "the New England Societies" at several points was signalized by this missile:

"The New England Society in the city of New York to the New England Society in Montreal, greeting: Thanks for your generous wishes. We shall not cease to labor for their complete fulfillment; and by the blessing of God, and our *still victorious arms*, we *mean* in our next anniversary, *in all the States, from Maine to California*, to celebrate the national jubilee in honor of the eternal *principles of liberty under the law,* which the Pilgrims, emerging from the cabin of the Mayflower, laid down as the corner stone of the nation."

This promised glorification is not to be for the restored union of the States, the vindicated authority of the Constitution and laws of the United States, and the return of peace and good will to a torn and warring people, but for the violent and revolutionary overthrow of slavery in all the slave States, in disregard of constitutional guarantees and the sanction and protection of laws, by the victorious armies of the United States. I suppose that this grandiloquent piece of fustian and falsehood is the emanation of some half crazed Massachusetts brain. Never was there a more impudent pharisaism uttered than that the *eternal principles of liberty under the law* were laid down as the *corner-stone* of the nation by the *Pilgrims* emerging

12

from the cabin of the Mayflower. The persecutions of Roger Williams and his Anabaptist associates, and the cropping of the Friends, the burning of witches, the most vexatious and tyrannical body of laws and regulations extending to the minutiæ of private and domestic life, and the long, habitual, and continuing disregard by Massachusetts of constitutions, laws, and treaties, all proclaim it to be untrue. Her early establishment by law of negro slavery, her enactment of the first and a vigorous fugitive slave law and slave code, declare its bold untruth.

The Mayflower landed her Pilgrims on Plymouth rock in 1620; and the Massachusetts Legislature, called "the General Court," in 1641, established this law:

"It is ordered by this court, and the authority thereof, that there shall never be any bond slavery, villainage, or captivity among us, *unless it be lawful captives taken* in just wars, *as willingly sell themselves* or *are sold to us*, and such shall have the liberties and Christian usages which the law of God established in Israel concerning such persons doth mortally require: *Provided*, This *exempts none* from servitude who shall be adjudged thereto by authority."

On the 5th of September, 1672, "Articles of Confederation of the New England Colonies" were ordained at Plymouth. Section seven provides:

"It is also agreed if any servant run away from his master into any other of these confederated jurisdictions, that in such case, upon the *certificate of one magistrate* in the jurisdiction out of which said servant fled, or upon other due proof, the said servant shall be delivered to his master or any other that pursues and brings such *certificate or proof*."

Here was the first fugitive slave law of North America.

In 1683, the General Court passed a law concerning the right of men to sell themselves for debt; and providing that the court of the county should regulate the time of service, so that other creditors "should not be deprived of their fair share of the *man's lifetime*." As early as 1636 the General Court had declared that no "covenant servant in household with any other should hold office or vote."

In 1636, Massachusetts passed a law in relation to "covenant servants," the first section of which is:

"It is ordered that no servant shall be set free or have any lot until he have served out the time covenanted, under penalty of such fine as the quarter's court shall inflict, unless they see cause to remit the same."

This provision continued to be her law for upward of a century.

In June, 1703, she passed this law, from which it appears there were mulattoes in the land of the Pilgrim Fathers at a very early day as well as negro slaves:

An act relating to mulatto and negro slaves.

Whereas great charge and inconveniences have arisen to divers towns and places by the releasing and setting at liberty mulatto and negro slaves: For prevention whereof for the future,

Be it declared and enacted by his Excellency the Governor, Council, and Representatives, in General Court assembled, and by the authority of the same, That no mulatto or negro slave shall hereafter be manumitted, discharged, or set free, until sufficient security be given to the treasurer of the town or place where such person dwells, in a valuable sum, not less than fifty pounds, to secure and indemnify the town or place from all charge for or about such mulatto or negro, to be manumitted and set at liberty, in case he or she by sickness, lameness, or otherwise, be rendered incapable to support him or herself.

And no mulatto or negro hereafter manumitted shall be deemed or accounted free, for whom security shall not be given as aforesaid, but shall be the proper charge of their respective masters or mistresses, in case they stand in need of relief and support, notwithstanding any manumission or instrument of freedom to them made or given; and shall also be liable at all times to be put forth to service by the selectmen of the town.

We adopted that law in Kentucky pretty much in the same language and having essentially the same meaning

In October of the same year Massachusetts passed this other law:

An act to prevent disorders in the night.

Whereas great disorders, insolences, and burglaries are ofttimes raised and committed in the night time by Indians, negro and mulatto servants and slaves, to the disquiet and hurt of her Majesty's good subjects: For the prevention thereof,

Be it enacted by his Excellency the Governor, Council, and Representatives, in general court assembled, and by the authority of the same, That no Indian, negro or mulatto servant or slave, may presume to be absent from the families whereto they respectively belong, or be found abroad in the night time after nine o'clock, unless it be upon some errand for their respective masters or owners. And all justices of the peace, constables, tithingmen, watchmen, and other her Majesty's good subjects, being householders within the same town, are hereby respectively empowered to take up and apprehend, or cause to be apprehended any Indian, negro or mulatto servant or slave that shall be found abroad after nine o'clock at night, and shall not give a good and satisfactory account of their business, make any disturbances or otherwise misbehave themselves, and forthwith convey them before the next justice of the peace, if it be not over late in the night, or to restrain them in the common prison, watch-house, or constable's house until the morning, and then cause them to appear before a justice of the peace, who shall order them to the house of correction to receive the discipline of the house, and then be dismissed; unless they be charged with any other offence than absence from the families whereto they respectively belong, without leave from their respective masters or owners; and in such towns where there is no house of correction to be openly whipped by the constable, not exceeding ten stripes.

In 1718 she passed a law to punish any master of a vessel who should receive on board a *hired servant* without permission of his master, and making him also liable in damages to the "master or owner." Within twenty years after the landing of the Mayflower the Pilgrim Fathers passed a law of which section three reads:

"Sec. 3. It is also ordered that when any servant shall run away from their masters" * * * "It shall be lawful for the next magistrate, or the constable and two of the chief inhabitants. where no magistrate is, to press men and boats or pinnaces at the public charge to pursue such persons by sea and land, and bring them back by force of arms."

Such are the laws and usages of Massachusetts, which established, regulated, and gave security to slave property, and that seem to have been the models upon which the more southern slaveholding colonies fashioned their laws in relation to the same subject. But the Massachusetts system was the more atrocious in several features: it comprehended *white men, Indians, negroes,* and *mulattoes.* The title of the masters was by importation from foreign countries, captivity in war, and purchase. It established a *servitude* by the sale of himself of the white man, and forbade his enfranchisement by his master until his term had expired. It enacted an effective fugitive slave law for the white man, Indian, mulatto, and negro, servant and slave; and when they eloped from their "owners and masters," authorized their pursuit at the public charge, and upon a *simple official certificate* of their being *slaves* or *servants,* and directed them to be returned to their *slavery* or *servitude.* It required not the *testimony of two witnesses,* and no *sworn evidence* whatever upon the point. It allowed no *trial* or *examination* before court or commissioner, no writ of *habeas corpus,* and *no bail* nor writ of replevin for the pursued fugitive; but its stern judgment was that he should go back into his former servitude or slavery. It punished the servant or slave, whether white, Indian, negro, or mulatto, male or female, with stripes, to be inflicted at the house of correction or publicly, for disorderly conduct or being from home after nine o'clock at night, unless on some special errand.

But, Mr. President, I now proceed to some of the minutiæ of Massachusetts slavery, as established by her early history. I quote from the Historical Magazine:

"Hugh Peter writes to John Winthrop from Salem (in 1637)"—

only seventeen years after the landing of the Mayflower—

"Mr. Endecot and my selfe salute you in the Lord Jesu, &c. Wee have heard of a dividence of women and children in the bay, and would be glad of a share, viz: a young woman or girle and a boy if you thinke good I wrote to you for some boyes tor Bermudas, which I think is considerable" (M H. S. Coll, 1V, vi, 95

In this application of Hugh Peter we have a glimpse of the beginning of the colonial slave trade. He wanted "some boyes for the Bermudas," which he thought was "considerable."

It would seem to indicate that this disposition of captive Indian boys was in accordance with custom and previous practice of the authorities. At any rate, it is certain that in the Pequod war they took many prisoners. Some of those who had been "disposed of to particular persons in the country," (Winthrop, I, 232,) ran away, and being brought in again were "branded on the shoulder." (Ib)

In May, 1637, Winthrop says:

"We had now slain and taken, in all, about seven hundred. We sent fifteen of the boys and two women to Bermuda by Mr Peirce; but he, missing it, carried them to Providence Isle." (Winthrop, I, 234.)

The learned editor of Winthrop's Journal, referring to the fact that this proceeding in that day was probably justified by reference to the practice or institution of the Jews, very quaintly observes, "Yet that cruel people never sent prisoners so far." (Ib., note.)

A subsequent entry in Winthrop's Journal gives us another glimpse of the subject, December 26, 1637:

"Mr. Peirce, in the Salem ship, the Desire, returned from the West Indies after seven months. He had been at Providence, and brought some cotton, and tobacco, and negroes, &c., from thence, and salt from Tertugos." (Ib., 254.)

Winthrop adds to this account that "dry fish and strong liquors are the only commodities for those parts. He met there two men-of-war, sent forth by the lords, &c., of Providence with letters of mart, who had taken divers prizes from the Spaniard and many negroes." Long afterwards Dr. Belknap said of the slave trade that the rum distilled in Massachusetts was "the mainspring of this traffick." (M. H S Coll., I, iv, 197)

Josselyn says, "That they sent the male children of the Pequots to the Bermudas." (258 M. H. S. Coll, IV, iii, 360.)

In the Pequot war, some of the Narragansetts joined the English in its prosecution, and received a part of the prisoners as slaves, for their services Miantonnomoh received eighty Ninigret was to have twenty. (Drake, 122, 146 Mather's Relation, quoted by Drake, 39. See also Hartford Treaty, September 21, 1638, in Drake, 125.)

Captain Stoughton, who assisted in the work of exterminating the Pequots, after his arrival in the enemy's country, wrote to the Governor of Massachusetts [Winthrop] as follows: "By this pinnace, you shall receive forty-eight or fifty women and children." * * * "Concerning which, there is one I formerly mentioned that is the fairest and largest that I saw amongst them, to whom I have given a coate to clothe her. It is my desire to have her for a servant, if it may stand with your good liking, else not."

I reckon that would have been the desire of the two Senators from Massachusetts if they had been there, especially of the gentleman who stands at the head of the Military Committee.

"There is a little squaw that Steward Culacut desireth, to whom he hath given a coate. Lieut. Davenport also desireth one, to wit, a small one, that hath three strokes upon her stomach, thus: — Ill -l-. He desireth her, if it will stand with your liking. Sosomon, the Indian, desireth a young little squaw, which I know not." (MS. Letter in Mass. Archives, quoted by Drake, 171.)

Probably if he had known her Sosomon would not have had the privilege of getting her.

An early traveler in New England has preserved for us the record of one of the earilest, if not indeed, the very first attempt at breeding of slaves in America. The following passage from Josselyn's Account of Two Voyages to New England, published at London in 1664, will explain itself.

"The second of October, [1639,] about 9 of the clock in the morning, Mr. Maverick's Negro woman came to my chamber window, and in her own Countrey language and tune sang very loud and shrill; going out to her, she used a great deal of respect towards me, and willingly would have expressed her grief in English; but I apprehended it by her countenance and deportment, whereupon I repaired to my host, to learn of him the cause, and resolved to intreat him in her behalf, for that I understood before, that she had been a Queen in her own Countrey, and observed a very humble and dutiful garb used towards her by another Negro who was her maid."

You see the term "negro" was used in that day. This fashionable shilly-shally language of "colored persons" and "descendant of Africa" was rather too circumlocutory, [laughter,] and they come out with the plain and direct term of "negro."

"Mr. Maverick was desirous to have a breed of Negroes, and therefore seeing she would not yield by persuasions to company with a Negro young man he had in his house; he commanded him will'd she nill'd she to go to bed to her, which was no sooner done but she kickt him out again, this she took in high disdain beyond her slavery, and this was the cause of her grief." (Josselyn, 28.)

What a nice specimen of a Puritan "consecrated to human liberty" have we here!

Emanuel Downing, a lawyer of the Inner Temple, London, who married Lucy Winthrop, sister of the older Winthrop, came over to New England in 1638 The editors of the Winthrop Papers say of him, "There were few more active or efficient friends of the Massachusetts Colony during its earliest and most critical period." His son was the famous Sir George Downing, English Embassador at the Hague.

In a letter to his brother-in-law, "probably written during the summer of 1645," is a most luminous illustration of the views of that day and generation on the subject of human slavery. He says:

"A warr with the Narragansett is verie considerable to this plantation, for I doubt whither yt be not synne in vs. hauing power in our hands, to suffer them to maynteyne the worship of the devil"—

Massachusetts-like. They wanted slaves then, and in order to make slaves of the Narragansetts, fanatical-like they took up the idea that they would make war because the Narragansetts worshipped the devil. I think Massachusetts has been guilty of a good deal of that sort of worship since. But to continue this extract:

"'which their paw wawes often doe; 2lie, If upon a Just warre the Lord should deliver them into our hands, wee might easily haue men, woemen and children enough to exchange for Moores, which wilbe more gayneful pilladge for us than wee conceive, for I do not see how wee can thrive untill wee gett into a stock of slaues sufficient to doe all our buisiness, for our children's children will hardly see this great Continent filled with people, soe that our servants will still desire freedom to plant for themselves, and not stay but for verie great wages. And I suppose you know verie well how wee shall maynteyne 20 Moores cheaper than one Englishe servant.'"

A matter of domestic economy entered largely into the subject. They could make valuable exchanges of Indian captives for Moors, a sort of negroes, and this writer says that one white servant was more expensive to his master than twenty Moors.

"The ships that shall bring Moores may come home laden with salt which may beare most of the chardge, if not all of yt. But I marvayle Conecticott should any wayes basard a warre without your helpe. (M. H. S. Coll., IV, vi, 65.) E. Y. E."

You see there the Massachusetts thrift. They wanted to put the whole cost of the voyage upon part of the cargo, so that the slaves they intended to purchase should not bear any portion of it.

Rev. Dr. Belknap, of Boston, Massachusetts, in a letter to Judge Tucker, of Williamsburg, Virginia, in 1795, admits the existence of negro slavery in Massachusetts, and that the slave trade was prosecuted by merchants in Massachusetts. He says that "the slaves purchased in Africa were chiefly sold in the West Indies, or in the Southern Colonies; but when these markets were glutted, and the price low, some of them were brought hither." He says, the slaves were most numerous in Massachusetts about 1745, and amounted to about 1 to 40 of the whites; and probably numbered about 4,000 or 5,000.*

* Mass. His. Collections, Volume IV, pp. 191—211.

In 1705, by another act, slaves were, for certain offences, to be sold out of the province. Any negro or mulatto, who should strike any of the English or other Christian nation, was to be severely whipped. Marriages were to be allowed between slaves, but I have found no law prohibiting a husband and wife from being sold apart. An import duty on negroes of £4 per head was imposed, but the duty was to be paid back, if the negro was exported, and "*bona fide* sold in any other plantation." "And the like advantages of the drawback shall be allowed to the purchaser of any negro sold within the Province."

In 1707, we find an act punishing free negroes or mulattoes, for harboring any negro or mulatto servant. And in 1718, an act imposed a penalty on every master of a vessel who should carry away any person under age, or *bought* or hired servant, without the master's or parent's consent. All these laws are to be found in the old folio volumes of Provincial Statutes.

"The Provincial Congress of Massachusetts prohibited the enlistment of slaves in the army; thus showing that slavery legally existed there in May, 1775. The reason given is a curious one—that they were contending for the liberties of the Colonies, and the admission into the army of any others but freemen, would be inconsistent with the principles to be supported, and reflect dishonor on the Colony."[*]

"In the year 1657, (during the reign of Endicott,) Lawrence Southwick, and Cassandra, his wife, very aged members of the Church in Salem, Massachusetts, for offering entertainment to two Quakers, were fined and imprisoned. They absented themselves from meeting, and were fined and whipped. A son and daughter of this aged, and according to Puritan standard, pious couple, were also fined for non-attendance at meeting; and not paying this fine, the General Court, by a special order, empowered the Treasurer *to sell them as slaves to any of the English nation at Virginia or Barbadoes.*"[†]

Mr. Samuel G. Drake, in his History of Boston, says that "many Irish people had been sent to New England," and sold as "slaves or servants." Also, that "many of the Scotch people had been sent, before this, in the same way. Some of them had been taken prisoners, at the sanguinary battle of Dunbar. There arrived in one ship, the 'John and Sara,' John Greene, master, early in the Summer of 1652, about 272 persons. Captain Greene had orders to deliver them to Thomas Kemble, of Charlestown, who was to sell them, and, with the proceeds, to take freight for the West Indies."[‡]

It is thus shown that negro slavery was a Massachusetts institution. In the Convention which formed the Constitution, the committee of detail reported the form of one with this clause:

" No tax or duty shall be laid by the Legislature on articles exported from any State; nor on the migration or importation of such persons as the several States shall think proper to admit; nor shall such migration or importation be prohibited."

If that provision had been retained, or if one authorizing Congress to prohibit the slave trade had not been adopted, any State could have continued it indefinitely. The people of Massachusetts were at that time largely and profitably engaged in the slave trade to the southern States. Luther Martin, of Maryland, proposed to amend the section as reported, so as to allow a prohibition or tax on the importation of slaves to be imposed by Congress. The members from Massachusetts divided on this proposition of Luther Martin. That section, with others, was referred to a committee of eleven, but Massachusetts failed to vote on the motion to refer, and that committee reported in lieu of it a provision authorizing Congress to prohibit the slave trade after the beginning of the year 1800. Mr. Pinckney, of South Carolina, moved to strike out 1800 and insert 1808. That motion prevailed, Massachusetts voting in favor of it; and thus by her position the slave trade would have been allowed to continue in perpetuity; but other States controlling her on that point, she was enabled to procure a continuance of it for twenty years longer. She, and all the States, voted for the provision authorizing the rendition of fugitive slaves. To that, which she now opposes with phrensied passion, there was no objection in the Convention. Her course is explained by the fact that the slave trade was *her trade.* She furnished the ships and sailors that visited the slave marts on the African coast and purchased negro captives from their savage conquerors for rum and trinkets, and carried them to the southern States and sold them for enriching prices in gold. She voted to continue her trade in slaves.

* Hon. E. R. Potter's Speech in the Senate of Rhode Island, March 14, 1868.
† Lambert's History of Colony at New Haven, p. 187.
‡ History and Antiquities of Boston, 1855, p. 342.

If Massachusetts had been situated in the low latitudes, and her soil had been rich, inexhaustible alluvion, producing cotton, sugar, and rice, who doubts that she would have been heavily peopled with African slaves, that she would now have held and would continue to hold on to them with the firm grip which has ever characterized the spirit of her all-covetousness, that she would to this day have been intensely pro-slavery; and that her two Senators, if under that state of things they could have got to the Senate, would be her most faithful representatives; and that she and they would now be resisting vehemently and obstinately such assaults upon the institution as they are making upon it? Massachusetts has always been active, energetic, alert, inventive, intellectual, avaricious, intermeddling, fanatical, domineering; but her love of acquisition has ever been and still is her master passion. She continued illicitly the slave trade after the law of Congress prohibiting it went into operation, and when it was finally broken up by the combined action of Congress, courts, and cruisers, and could no longer minister to her rapacity by the smuggling of slaves into the southern States her more subordinate characteristics, fanaticism and meddlesomeness, began to spring up, and after a while became dominant. She conceived the project of robbing the people of the southern States of the slaves that she had carried and sold to them for money. In the name of a spurious philanthropy she commenced to agitate in every form most industriously and intensely to distroy that property, not in Cuba and Brazil, but among her own countrymen and customers, and set up her impudent and absurd "higher law" conceits to break down the constitutional and legal guarantees with which it had been so long environed, and which she contributed so much to build up. She inaugurated not only in her own borders, but in every locality to which her people could gain access, a general system of talking, lecturing, declaiming, and preaching against the "great crime of slavery," publishing newspapers, tracts, novels, essays,. books, and pictures, all fraught with the basest falsehoods and slanders against it and slaveowners, and rendering and intending to render it abhorrent to the northern people.

Massachusetts thus estranged, divided, and exasperated the people of the free and slave States. She, with malice aforethought, schooled them to hate each other with a diabolical purpose of sundering the Union and subverting the Constitution because of the protection which it gave to the owners of slaves. She complained that the freedom of speech and the press and her rights were violated because the slave States would not open their bosoms to her nefarious agitation of that property, and of the right upon which it was founded. Let us look at her deliberate resolves.

Mr. WILKINSON. If the Senator from Kentucky will permit me, I will move an adjournment.

Mr. DAVIS. Well, this is a pretty good stopping place.

Mr. WILKINSON. I wish to move an adjournment: but before doing so, I ask the Senate to take up Senate bill No. 41, to promote enlistments in the Army of the United States, and for other purposes, with a view to make it the special order for Thursday next, at one o'clock.

The VICE PRESIDENT. That motion will be entertained by the unanimous consent of the Senate. If there be no objection, that will be regarded as the sense of the Senate, and that bill will be assigned for Thursday next, at one o'clock, and be made the special order for that hour. The question now is on an adjournment.

The motion was agreed to; and the Senate adjourned.

Mr. DAVIS on the next day resumed his remarks as follows:

Mr. PRESIDENT: A philosopher and a poet once published a couplet:

"For forms of government let fools contest;
That which is best administered is best."

There is more truth and philosophy than poetry in that couplet. In point of excellence and perfection of form there is no Government that ever had existence which is equal to ours; but in its administration at this time I believe that it is one of the most oppressive and grinding that now exists. I think it is practically a military despotism. There is no constitutional provision, there is no law of Congress, there is no constitution or law of a State but what crumbles in its presence and at its touch.

The Constitution of the United States establishes the judicial department of the Government. It refers all questions of a judicial character, whether arising under the Constitution or the law, to that department for its decision. There is no right of the citizen, whether it be personal, appertaining to his life and his liberty, or his property, but what is legitimately the subject of the inquiry and judgment of the judicial department of the Government. But in this day of usurpation of power and of practical revolution these provisions of the Constitution and the law are wholly disregarded; and the President of the United States, under a claim of military necessity, repudiates and sweeps away the whole Constitution and all the laws of Congress, and all the civil tribunals appointed by the Constitution and the law for their enforcement, and in their stead he substitutes, by his own arbitrary will, military courts, and makes the indefinite and indefinable law of their own will the rule of their proceedings, action, and judgments, instead of the ordinary and civil law by which to adjudge and punish the citizen.

There is no man whose rights are safe from the assaults of the Government of the United States at this time. There is no man whose property is not subject to be taken from him by the arbitrary action of some subordinate military officer, without compensation, without any proper inquiry for the purpose of deciding whether there is a state of case in which such power may be rightfully exercised. There is no provision made by law to remunerate the owner of property for that which is thus arbitrarily taken from him. The writ of *habeas corpus* is suspended; and on that point I will remark that the only proper effect of it is to prevent the citizen from having that summary and *ex parte* examination of his case that is incident to the return and to the hearing of the writ. The suspension of the writ does not properly arrest or suspend or obstruct the legal trial by the proper civil court, which every citizen is entitled to have according to the guarantee of the Constitution; and any courts which lend themselves to the purpose of suspending the due administration of the law by refusing such trials, make themselves criminally subservient to the same usurpation of power.

There is no citizen of the United States, even in the loyal States, but what is subject, at all times, to be arrested at any hour of the day or the night, without any process issued out according to the requisitions of the Constitution, without any charge of offense or crime, without its being communicated to him what is the cause of his arrest; and he is subject to be dragged from his home to distant prisons, and there to be indefinitely confined in a dungeon without any protection or redress.

Sir, under our form of constitutional government, and of its limited and restricted jurisdiction, in addition to the abuses which I have enumerated, all the State laws of every State, loyal as well as disloyal, are subject to be superseded by the arbitrary will of the President and his military subordinates; courts are deposed; judges are driven from their balls; ministerial officers with process in their hands are interdicted from making execution of them; and armed men invade the courts for the purpose of suppressing the due execution of law and defeating the protection which should be vouchsafed to every citizen.

Sir, not only all this abuse; but when the wave of rebellion is driven back from some of the States, and our conquering armies have taken or are about to take undisputed possession of those reconquered States, the President of the United States assumes the unconstitutional and dictatorial power to prohibit those States from returning to the Union under their constitutions and laws. He imposes upon them conditions which he has no more authority or power to impose than you or I have, and he requires that these conditions shall be complied with by their people before they shall be admitted to their constitutional rights as States of this Confederacy, and the people of those States to the protection, the rights, and the liberties guarantied to them by the Federal Constitution and laws and their own States' constitutions and laws.

Sir, under the impression produced upon my mind by this hasty and imperfect review, I come to the conclusion, and I here declare in my place my solemn conviction, that the despotism of Russia or of Austria is not so oppressive, so galling, and so grinding as the military despotism that is now in full operation in the United States. This military despotism has been but partially executed. Reëlect the incumbent who now fills the presidential chair, or elect a man of the same or more extreme principles and policy, and you then confirm by the vote of the people of the United States the present usurpations of those in power, their assumptions of that enormous and tyrannical power that never was intended to be, and never was in fact, delegated to them by the framers of the Constitution, and which if it had been proposed would have produced a prompt rejection by that body unanimously, I have no doubt, if it had not broken up the body itself without accomplishing its work.

Sir, what said, as reported in the papers, our Secretary of State to the British minister, Lord Lyons? "My lord, I can touch a bell on my right hand and order the arrest of a citizen of Ohio; I can touch the bell again and order the imprisonment of a citizen of New York; and no power on earth except that of the President can release him. Can the Queen of England do as much?" No, sir; nor the Emperor Napoleon, nor the Emperor Alexander, nor any other potentate of the earth, can enact the same despotism that is expressed in this brief but most true and most terrible picture of arbitrary power.

Mr. ANTHONY. Allow me to ask the Senator from Kentucky when such remarks were made by the Secretary of State?

Mr. DAVIS. I have just stated that all I know about it is its publication in the newspapers

Mr. ANTHONY. Does the Senator deem that sufficient authority on which to present such a statement to the Senate?

Mr. DAVIS. I should be gratified to find that it was not true; but if it not true I should suppose the Secretary of State would contradict it.

Mr. ANTHONY. I leave the Senator himself to decide whether it is not more proper to find out that a statement is true before he quotes it in the Senate.

Mr. DAVIS. Here is the report of a most extraordinary declaration by the Secretary of State to the minister of the first Power on earth accredited to our Government. This declaration is published in the papers, and, so far as I know and have understood, it never has been contradicted.

Mr. ANTHONY. I will ask if the Senator from Kentucky——

Mr. DAVIS. Let me proceed, if you please. Make a memorandum of your questions, and present them to me when I get through. I would rather answer them altogether.

Mr. ANTHONY. The only question I wish to ask is whether the Senator himself is in the habit of contradicting the remarks he finds in the newspapers about himself, or are we to believe everything that we see about him in the papers which he does not contradict?

Mr. DAVIS. If I were Secretary of State, and such a remark as that were made about my communications to Lord Lyons, the British minister, and it was not true, I certainly would contradict it.

But, Mr. President, I proceed now in the line of my remarks. It is not my purpose to occupy any more time than is necessary, and I do not wish to trouble the Senate again at any length. I know the Senate are weary with hearing me, and, to acknowledge the God's truth, I am beginning to be really wearied of hearing myself. [Laughter.]

Mr. President, when I yielded the floor yesterday I had advanced to that stage in the history and the progress of action by the great State of Massachusetts when she had reversed all her former principles and positions on the subject of slavery, And now let me read of some public action and resolves of that State in support of this new and most extraordinary, unconstitutional, illegal, and unjust policy upon which she has entered with so much vim. A convention was held in Boston in 1855 that unanimously adopted resolutions which I will read:

"*Resolved*, That a Constitution which provides for a slave representation and a slave oligarchy in Congress, which legalizes slave-hunting and slave-catching on every inch of American soil, and which pledges the military and naval power of the country to keep four million chattel slaves in their chains, is to be trodden under foot and pronounced accursed, however unexceptionable and valuable its other provisions may be."

When Massachusetts was fulminating such a denunciation as that against the Constitution, why did she not recollect and why was she not brought to shame and to dumbness by her previous course in relation to the same subject? Why was she not struck mute by her course in the Convention which formed the Constitution of the United States? Why did she denounce a provision of the Constitution that was passed by the unanimous support of the members of the Convention, including her own, that provision which secures to the owners of fugitive slaves their rendition from other States into which they may have escaped?

The next resolution of this series is:

"*Resolved*, That the one great issue before the country is the dissolution of the Union, in comparison with which all other issues with the slave power are as dust in the balance; therefore we will give ourselves to the work of annulling this 'covenant with death' as essential to our own innocency and the speedy and everlasting overthrow of the slave system."

Sir, gentlemen get up now and flippantly and audaciously hurl the charge of treason at other members of the Senate, and at true and loyal citizens over the land—men who have uttered this treasonable sentiment, men who have cherished it as the purpose and object of their lives and of their policy. In January, 1857, Massachusetts held a State convention at Worcester, that passed the resolutions that I will now read:

19

"*Resolved,* That this movement does not seek merely disunion, but the more perfect union of the free States by the expulsion of the slave States from the confederation in which they have ever been an element of discord, danger, and disgrace."

There is a slight mistake. The true subject of that denunciation should have been, not the slave States, but the State of Massachusetts herself. "Give the devil his due." Speak of South Carolina and the other States that are now in this wicked rebellion, and when, and where, and how did they ever interfere with the constitutions and laws of the northern or free States, with their domestic institutions, with their rights of property, with any of those interests or affairs that were left to them by the Constitution and over which they had the exclusive jurisdiction? The southern States never intermeddled in the domestic concerns of Massachusetts or any of the other northern States; and if Matsachusetts had herself acted with the the same forbearance, with the same scrupulous regard to the provisions and the spirit of the Constitution of the United States and to the great principles upon which our system, State and Federal, is based, we should not now have this deplorable war upon us.

The next resolution was:

"*Resolved,* That it is not probable that the ultimate severance of the Union will be an act of deliberation or discussion, but that a long period of deliberation and discussion must precede it; and this we meet to begin."

They mean to begin for the diabolical purpose of agitating with a view to the dissolution of the Union! Was there ever so treasonable an avowal so boldly made by any body of men?

"*Resolved,* That henceforward, instead of regarding it as an objection to any system of policy, that it will lead to the separation of the States, we will proclaim that to be the highest of all recommendations and the greatest proof of statesmanship; and we will support, politically or otherwise, such men and measures as appear to tend most to this result.

"*Resolved,* That by the repeated confession of northern and southern statesmen, 'the existence of the Union is the chief guaranty of slavery;' and that the despots of the whole world have everything to fear, and the slaves of the whole world everything to hope, from its destruction and the rise of a free northern republic

"*Resolved,* That the sooner the separation takes place the more peaceful it will be; but that peace or war is a secondary consideration in view of our present perils. Slavery must be conquered, 'peaceably if we can, forcibly if we must.'"

That principle they then took up and they are now acting fully up to its execution, not by the power of Massachusetts alone, but by the aggregate power of the vast armies of the United States.

"*Resolved,* That the experience of more than sixty years has proved our national Government to be a mere creature and tool of the slave power."

How? Had not the free States preponderated in the two Houses of Congress and in the electoral college which made the President and Vice President ever since the beginning of the Government? Had they not always the power and the strength to make whom they willed President and Vice President, and to pass such laws as they chose? Then the course of presidential elections and of congressional legislation was the judgment and the act of the free States, at least so many of them and such of their representatives and electors as when united with those from the slave States, gave them power. But my recollection both of legislation and of presidential elections is that never until sectional parties grew up in the United States were there any divisions of that kind in relation to any subject of policy and legislation, or in the election of President and Vice President; but it was always a mixed vote of free and slave States, without a division and separation by the line of slavery.

"*Resolved,* That the experience of more than sixty years has proved our national Government to be a mere creature and tool of the slave power, subservient only to the purpose of despotism; a formidable obstacle to the advancement and prosperity both of the free and slave States; a libel upon our democratic theories of government; a disgrace to the civilization of the age, and a bitter curse to the cause of freedom in our own country and throughout the world."

Did not every point and subject of this bitter malediction exist at the time that the Convention framed our present Constitution? Did they not all exist at the era of the Declaration of Independence, and when it was recognized by the treaty of 1783? Were not all these matters that are thus bitterly denounced, originated, built up, and sustained by the action of Massachusetts? These resolutions proceed:

"*Resolved,* That, in view of this long and painful experience, we have no longer any hope of its reformation, but are fully convinced that the best interests of every section of the country require its immediate dissolution.

"*Resolved,* That this convention recommends, as the first step toward the accomplishment of this object, the organization in each of the States of a political party outside of the present Constitution and Union—a party whose candidates shall be publicly pledged, in the event of their election, to ignore the Federal Government, to refuse an oath to its Constitution, and to make their respective States free and independent communities."

Sir, was there ever a fouler or more audacious position of disloyalty to our Government, a bolder and more daring disregard of the obligation which every citizen owed to the Government, than is manifested in this series of resolutions? Now, I will read some of the mottoes inscribed upon the banners of this dissolution party in the State of Massachusetts and other States who are members of the loyal leagues and making such lofty claims of unconditional support of the Union:

"Thorough organization and independent political action on the part of the non-slaveholding whites of the South. Ineligibility of slaveholders. Never another vote to the traffickers in human flesh.

"No patronage to slaveholding merchants; no guests to slaveholding hotels; no fees to slaveholding lawyers; no employment to slaveholding physicians; no audience to slaveholding parsons; no recognition of pro-slavery men except as ruffians, outlaws, and criminals.

"Immediate death to slavery, or, if not immediate, unqualified proscription of its advocates during the period of its existence."

Was there ever a fiercer, a more savage and unrelenting war denounced against any institution or any set of men who were faithfully sustaining their Government and laws, their only sin being the adoption of slavery, an institution founded by Massachusetts?

The descendants of those men now turn upon an institution which they fostered and carried to and enlarged in the Southern States by the slave traffic, in their own ships and with their own capital. Is it not one of the most extraordinary and extreme inconsistencies ever exhibited to mankind? Could any race of people except the descendants of the Pilgrim Fathers be guilty of it?

Mr. President, Massachusetts in 1843 passed her first law in direct hostility to the fugitive slave law of 1793. This last law was enacted in obedience to an express provision of the Constitution, that persons held to slavery in one State escaping into another should be rendered back to their owners. That provision of the Constitution was as valid and as obligatory on the people of Massachusetts and their Senators as any provision in that instrument. The law was passed when Washington was President, and by a Congress many of whose members had been engaged in the revolutionary struggle and had been members of the Federal Convention. It was passed in the Senate without a division, and in the House of Representatives by a vote of 58 to 7. It came under the revision of the courts of the United States, and of the States, and it was sustained by every judicial tribunal, Federal and State. It was approved by the Father of his Country, the man at the head of the human race, who rises high above every other specimen of humanity notwithstanding he was a slaveholder, and who in all his attributes and his whole life was more godlike than any man that has appeared upon earth since the days of the inspired apostles.

Shortly after Congress had passed the second fugitive slave law, in 1850, there was formed in Boston an association that combined talent, wealth, office, position, numbers and permaneney, for the special and declared purpose, and by all means even unto organized armed resistance, to defeat any and all attempts to execute the fugitive slave laws in that State, and now her paramount and darling purpose in the vehement support she gives to the war, is not for restoration, but revolutionary and violent overthrow of slavery and the organism of the slave States, and virtually of the Union and Constitution of the United States, by making their armies the instrument of this her work of destruction.

Will the Senator from Massachusetts at the head of the Military Committee state on this floor that he never had knowledge of that association in the city of Boston and of the special and isolated object of its organization? Did he never meet with it in council? Was he never advised with by its leading and active members? Did he never give it his countenance and support? The other Senator from Massachussetts is too open I presume to deny his position in relation to that organization, but his more covert colleague is dumb and silent in relation to these points of interrogatory. But I will proceed with what I was saying in regard to Massachusetts Her most sinister, selfish, and wicked ends are in that way to get possession of the rich cotton and sugar lands and the freed negroes of the Southern States, and work them in perpetuity for the emolument of the sons of the Pilgrim Fathers; to reduce the Southern States to a sort of colonial dependence, and to make them industrially, commercially, and politically subservient to herself and the northern States.

That is the whole scheme, combining fanaticism, avarice, meddlesomeness, and all the other obnoxious characteristics that appertain to that peculiar people, the descendents of the Pilgrim Fathers.

I have before me a life of the fugitive slave Burns written by Stevens, a Massachusetts man. After speaking of the public excitement produced in Boston by that arrest, he adds:

"No immediate step was taken, however, except by an association styled a committee of vigilance. This association took its origin from the passage of the fugitive slave act. *Its sole object was to defeat in all cases the execution of that hated Statute.* Thoroughly organized under a written code of laws, with the necessary officers and working committees, arranged on the principle of a subdivision of labor, with wealth and professional talent at its command, actuated by the most determined purpose and operating in secret, it was well fitted to strike powerful blows for the accomplishment of *its* object."

The object was the defeat and the overthrow of an act of Congress by a bold and treasonable band of conspirators, which, if successful, would have been *pro tanto* a dissolution of the Union; and yet men who support and give their presence and countenance and aid to such organization for such a purpose, have the face to come here and take an oath to support the Constitution of the United States, which this whole movement was intended to strike down in part, and to brand as disloyal and semi-traitorous men more true and loyal to the Government and to every principle of good faith than they. The historian further says of this association:

"The roll of its members displayed the most diversified assemblage of characters, but this diversity only secured the greater efficiency. The white and the colored race, free-born sons of Massachusetts and fugitive slaves from the South here co-operated together. Among them were men of fine culture and of high social position. Some of the rich men of Boston were enrolled in this committee."

The historian then proceeds to give details of the many modes in which this organization operated. He adds:

"By this committee of vigilance the case of Burns was now taken in hand. Early in the afternoon of the day following his arrest a full meeting for the purpose was secretly convened "

For what purpose? To take Burns from the custody of the law, and in that way to repeal, practically to put down, the law of Congress. I read further:

"On the main point there was but one voice; all agreed that, be the commissioner's decision what it might, Burns should never be taken back to Virginia if it were in their power to prevent."

Burns was arrested on the 24th of May, 1854, and by the judgment of the commissioner was rendered up to his master the 2d of June. In that interval there was addressed a circular letter to the " yeomanry of Massachusetts" adjuring them to to rendezvous at Boston with a view to the case of Burns. Some three hundred men were organized in Worcester and marched to Boston, and large numbers from most of the adjacent towns concentrated there. Every sort of appeal was made by the leading friends of Burns to inflame and madden the people in his favor and to rescue him at any cost. One night it was estimated there were from eight to ten thousand infuriated men, and the most of them secretly armed, surrounding the court-house in which he was confined to coerce his release. To execute the fugitive slave law in his case about two thousand armed and drilled men, artillery, infantry, marines, and volunteers, had to be assembled to sustain the civil magistrates. But for that effective and large military force to sustain the civil officers, what would have become of the law of Congress and of the appointed magistrates for its execution? The whirlwind of passion and crime that then agitated Boston and rocked that city from its centre to its exterior would have swept these powerless officers from their posts and Burns would have been rescued and set free, and there would have been a practical revolution of the Government consummated, not total, but to the extent of the overthrow of an important policy and law of Congress, in which nearly half the States were deeply interested. If bold and daring treason had been successful, the Government would virtually have been brought to an end; its whole moral power would have been subverted; and it would have been contemned, not only in relation to that law, but to all others that the treasonable and wicked spirit of Massachusetts might have prompted her to resist.

On the second night after Burns' arrest, and before the forces to rescue him, or those to prevent it, had assembled in large numbers, a portion of his armed friends, led on by Rev. Thomas W. Higginson, made an assault on the court-house in which he was confined and guarded by United States soldiery, to wrest him from the custody of the law. The door was ponderous and strong, but, by a kind of catapult, the assailants broke out one of its panels, and Higginson and a few of his associate traitors made an entry. They were repelled, but it was said by Higginson; and a soldier was also wounded. Higginson was both a murderer and traitor, and, if possible should have been twice hung in expiation of each offense. But the present Executive has appointed him colonel of a negro regiment.

Sir what kind of a moral example is that? The President of the United States is sworn to uphold, defend, and protect the Constitution and to execute the laws, and yet he appoints a murderer and a traitor to be a colonel of one of the regiments now in the military service of the United States.

The Senator from Massachusetts—I mean the military Senator—did not answer but evaded the question whether "he was against the rescue of Burns," and replied, "I had nothing to do with it;" and repeated, "I had nothing to do with it, and had no knowledge of it until after it transpired. I was not in my own State at the time." And to the question, "Did you ever condemn that insurrection? Did you ever do anything to put it down—its spirit?" he would not answer directly, but evasively, thus: "There was no occasion; it was put down quickly."

At the time of the attempted rescue of Burns, did not that Senator know that there existed a powerful organization in Boston formed for no other purpose than to defeat the execution of the fugitive slave law as often as there should be an arrest under it? Was he ever counseled in relation to that association, and its object and *modus operandi?* Had he learned that this rescue would be attempted, and did he run away from his friends and comrades as he did from the battle of Bull Run, to avoid responsibility and danger? Natick, his place of residence, is, I believe, about seventeen miles from Boston. How came he to be away from his home and out of the State for more than nine days from the time Burns was arrested until he was rendered up and taken "back to old Virginny!" Where was he all that time? What was he doing? Is it not most strange that in more than nine days he should not have heard of this most exciting affair, the telegraph, too, being in operation? But the member from Massachusetts said of this demonstration to rescue Burns:

"The Senator [Mr. DAVIS] prates about a little mob composed of a few men in the city of Boston, and brands their action as insurrection and rebellion. Insurrection! Rebellion! Sir, there was no insurrection; there was no rebellion. It was at most but a mob, and a very small mob at that."

The Senator has become so greatly augmented that he has not only Cyclopean notions of *himself* but also of rebellions and insurrections. I have presented to the Senate the facts of the attempt to rescue Burns, as published in the newspapers at the time, and as they have since been recorded by a Boston historian. It was *one* outbreak of a numerous and powerful organization of conspirators and traitors, who had combined and confederated together to defy the authority of the United States, and by force of arms and all other means to defeat wholly and in all cases as they might arise the execution of their law. That organization had then existed for years, and I suppose still exists. It was much more formidable in its plan, arrangement, numbers, wealth, intelligence, duration, and in the force it displayed when the rescue was attempted than was the combination in Pennsylvania to defeat the execution of the law of Congress to levy an excise on whisky. That was at the time and now is in history denominated an insurrection, and so will and so ought the attempt to rescue Burns to be characterized, and if it had been successful would have been in fact a revolution of the Government by force of arms.

But, Mr. President, in the face of the facts which I have arrayed to the contrary, the member from Massachusetts has the effrontery to declare to the country in this Chamber that—

"No man in her Legislature desired or expected to resist the authority of the Federal Government. What Massachusetts intended to accomplish by her legislation was the protection of her *own citizens;* and if any question arose between her and the Federal Government, growing out of the attempted execution of the fugitive slave act, she was *ever ready* to submit those questions to the judicial tribunals of the country and to *abide* the verdict."

This position is both disingenuous and untrue. It attempts to make a discrimination between the *men in her Legislature* and her people, and to claim a special immunity for the former alone. All questions arising under the fugitive slave law, however the Legislature of Massachusetts might endeavor to draw those coming up in that State to her own courts, are by an express provision of the Constitution referred exclusively to the decision of the Federal courts. They had all been decided, again and again, by the Supreme Court and the circuit courts of the United States against her positions and assumptions. She would not abide by those decisions; and it was in a treasonable spirit and effort to reverse them, and practically to nullify the fugitive slave laws of Congress, that she passed what is called "her personal liberty bill," by which, against the Constitution of the United States, she sought to bring and retry all those questions in her own abolition courts and by her own abolition juries.

Was Burns and every other fugitive slave who might get to Boston citizens of Massachusetts? That is the position of the Senator and his State. Governor Andrew ostentatiously published that if Lincoln would make a proclamation of freedom to the slaves the roads and alleys would swarm with Massachusetts volunteers rushing to the war. Yet in a very short time afterwards the agents of Massachusetts, with the Senator's co-operation, were scouring the rebel and loyal States, the slave and the free States, offering large bounties for negro recruits, free, slave, and freedmen, to fill up her quota and keep her own white people from the war. Massachusetts is a great State, but her people have some queer notions, and always think their will ought to control. The member from Massachusetts says:

"Sir, the imputations, the reproaches, the slanders, that so glibly flow from the lips of the Senator from Kentucky will not reach the Commonwealth of Massachusetts. No word of his can soil her name or dim her fame. There is not strength enough to his arm to fling a shaft that shall strike that proud old Commonwealth."

The Senator attempts to pull on the buskins of Mr. Webster, and affects the terseness, dignity, and grandeur of his defense of Massachusetts against the assaults of Senator Hayne, of South Carolina. I advise *his successor* to quit his attempts to copy Mr. Webster; he only apes his model, and it is miserably bad apeing too; or some time when he is attempting to swell himself to the stature of Mr. Webster, the scene of the frog and the ox may be re-enacted. But I concede one of the positions tions of the member from Massachusetts: "No word of mine can soil her name or dim her fame." If she has not herself, or such of her degenerate sons as the have not soiled her name or dimmed her fame, they are safe from me. But let us examine that question a little further.

Her arrogant, dictatorial, and "rule-or-ruin" spirit broke forth in opposition to the acquisition of Louisiana during Mr. Jefferson's Administration, and she denounced the treaty by which that vast country was acquired, because of the want of constitutional power on the part of our Government to acquire foreign territory, and also of the impolicy of the measure. She made her similar arrogant condemnation of the treaty in which Spain ceded Florida to the United States. Throughout the war of 1812 with Great Britain, which was declared to protect Massachusetts seamen against impressment by that haughty Power, and to vindicate the freedom of the seas and the rights of international commerce, in which her people were so largely interested, that spirit became so heightened and deepened, so malignant and treasonable, as to break forth in the most vituperative condemnation of the war and our own Government by the people of Massachusetts; in frequent and most criminal attempts to thwart and defeat the United States in their great struggle to bring the war to a speedy and successful close; in a resort by them to manifold devices to weaken, dispirit, and produce the defeat of our land and naval forces, and to strengthen and give aid and comfort and victory to our enemy; in continual and most extravagant laudation of the policy, power, and moral position of England in that war, and the basest disparagement of their own country and Government by imputations of corruption and imbecility, of prejudice against England and subserviency to France, and a purpose, not to redress national wrongs, but of rapacity, ambition, and conquest; in efforts to detach the thirteen original States and leave the Federal Government and the other States at war with one of the greatest Powers of the earth; and another most absurd and wicked project, that New England should make a separate peace with Great Britain, and at the end of the war its States should resume their position in the United States. These are grave charges and most disparaging to Massachusetts, and it is to be deplored that they are true in their fullest force.

She elected a Governor and Legislature hostile to the Government of the United States and opposed to the war, and who exerted themselves continuously and defiantly to uphold the cause of England, and to coerce the President of the United States to make an ignominious treaty, without the concession or acknowledgment by Great Britain of a single right for which the war was undertaken.

Her people first got up the Essex Junto and then the Hartford Convention, both of which were treasonable associations, composed of the enemies of their own Government and the friends and sympathizers of England; and their objects and action were to divide our people, distract the public councils, weaken the military operations of the United States, and to make the war so disastrous as to force them to a shameful peace.

In the summer of 1812, some two months after the declaration of war, President Madison made a requisition on Governor Strong of that State for a portion of her militia to enter the service of the United States. He refused to comply; and in connection with his council submitted to the judges of the supreme court of that

State several questions which it will not be necessary to read, as they are embodied in the answers of the judges. Those answers I will read:

To his Excellency the Governor and the Honorable Council of the Commonwealth of Massachusetts :

The undersigned Justices of the supreme judicial court, have considered the several questions proposed by your Excellency and Honors for their opinion.

By the constitution of this State, the authority of commanding the militia of the Commonwealth is vested exclusively in the Governor, who has all the powers incident to the office of commander-in-chief, and is to exercise them personally, or by subordinate officers under his command, agreeably to the rules and regulations of the constitution and the laws of the land.

While the Governor of the Commonwealth remained in the exercise of these powers the Federal Constitution was ratified, by which was vested in the Congress a power to provide for calling forth the militia *to execute the laws of the Union, suppress insurrection, and repel invasions,* and to provide for governing such part of them as may be employed in the service of the United States. reserving to the States respectively the appointment of the officers. The Federal Constitution further provides that the President shall be Commander-in-Chief of the Army of the United States, and of the militia of the several States when called into the actual scrviee of the United States.

On the construction of the Federal and State constitutions must depend the answers to the several questions proposed. As the militia of the several States may be employed in the service of the United States for the three specific purposes of executing the laws of the Union, of suppressing insurrections, and repelling invasions, the opinion of the judges is requested whether the commanders-in-chief of the militia of the several States have a right to determine whether any of the exigencies aforesaid exist, so as to require them to place the militia, or any part of it, in the service of the United States, at the request of the President, to be commanded by him pursuant to acts of Congress.

It is the opinion of the undersigned that this right is vested in the commanders-in-chief of the militia of the several States.

The Federal Constitution provides that when either of these exigencies exist the militia may be employed, pursuant to some act of Congress, in the service of the United States; but no power is given, either to the President or to the Congress, to determine that either of the said exigencies does in fact exist. As this power is not delegated to the United States by the Federal Constitution nor prohibited by it to the States, it is reserved to the States respectively, and, from the nature of the power, it must be exercised by those with whom the States have respectively intrusted the chief command of the militia.

It is the duty of these commanders to execute this important trust agreeably to the laws of their several States respectively, without reference to the laws or officers of the United States in all cases except those specially provided for in the Federal Constitution. They must, therefore, determine when either of the special cases exist, obliging them to relinquish the execution of this trust, and to render themselves and the militia subject to the command of the President.

A different construction, giving to Congress the right to determine when those special cases exist, authorizing them to call forth the whole of the militia, and taking them from the commanders-in-chief of the several States and subjecting them to the command of the President, would place all the militia, in effect, at the will of Congress, and produce a military consolidation of the States, without any constitutional remedy, against the intentions of the people when ratifying the Federal Constitution. Indeed, since the passing of the act of Congress of February 28, 1795, vesting in the President the power of calling forth the militia when the exigencies mentioned in the Constitution shall exist, if the President has the power of determining when those exigencies exist, the militia of the several States is in fact at his command and subject to his control.

No inconveniences can reasonably be presumed to result from the construction which vests in the commanders-in-chief of the militia in the several States the right of determining when the exigencies exist obliging them to place the militia in the service of the United States. These exigencies are of such a nature that the existence of them can be easily ascertained by or made known to the commanders-in-chief of the militia; and, when ascertained, the public interest will induce a prompt obedience to the acts of Congress.

Another question proposed to the consideration of the justices is, whether, when either of the exigencies exist authorizing the employing of the militia in the service of the United States, the militia thus employed can be lawfully commanded by any officer but of the militia except by the President of the United States.

The Federal Constitution declares that the President shall be the Commander-in-Chief of the Army of the United States. He may undoubtedly exercise this command by officers of the Army of the United States, by him commissioned according to law. The President is also declared to be the Commander-in-Chief of the militia of the several States when called into the actual service of the United States. The officers of the militia are to be appointed by the States; and the President may exercise his command of the militia by the officers of the militia duly appointed. But we know of no constitutional provision authorizing any officer of the Army of the United States to command the militia, or authorizing any officer of the militia to command the Army of the United States. The Congress may provide laws for the government of the militia when in actual service; but to extend this power to the placing of them under the command of an officer not of the militia, except the President, would render nugatory the provision that the militia are to have officers appointed by the States.

The union of the militia in the actual service of the United States with the troops of the United States. so as to form one Army, seems to be a case not provided for or contemplated in the Constitution; &c.

Now, sir, this opinion decides two principles. It states correctly that there are three exigencies provided for by the Constitution in which the militia of the States may be called into the service of the United States: first, to execute the laws; second, to repel invasions; and third, to put down insurrection; but that opinion assumes as a constitutional principle that the power to decide when any or all these exigencies happens belongs not to Congress or to the President of the United States, but to the Governors of the States; and even when the Governors themselves have decided such an exigency to exist and have ordered their militia into the service of the United States, the militia can be commanded by no United States military officer, except by the President himself.

Sir, there is another specimen of Massachusetts loyalty: the Governor of Massachusetts having refused to order the militia of that State into the service of the United States, some of the patriotic people of the district of Maine volunteered, and were placed by the President under the command of General William King. In the year 1813 the Legislature of that State passed a resolution inquiring of General King whether he had accepted any agency or commission from the United States, or received from them any arms or munitions by order of the President of the United States. General King replied:

"The volunteers who tendered their services to the President for the defense of their country were accepted and organized; and have been furnished with arms on application to the General Government. Soon after the commencement of the present war, when the services of the detached militia were withheld from the General Government, I aided the War Department in organizing such a volunteer corps as was considered necessary for the defense of this district. After two regiments were organized, the services of such a number of companies were offered as would have made three other regiments, if necessary. As a citizen of the United States I have duties to perform as well as a citizen of the State, in this just and holy war."

A response worthy the friend of that often-tried and true patriot, John Holmes. Massachusetts afterwards asked and received pay, not for the services but for the time of the militia that she withheld from the United States in their second great struggle for independence.

This traitorous Governor Strong and his coadjutors in Massachusetts procured the weak and corrupt Governor of Vermont, Chittenden, to take *their* position, that it was the *exclusive right* of *the Governors* of the States to decide *whether* and *when* there existed an *exigency* that required the State militia to be put into the service of the United States, and to issue an infamous proclamation commanding the volunteer militia of Vermont to march back from Plattsburg, whither they had rushed to defend that place against the assault of one of the most formidable British armies that was assembled during the war. The traitors of Massachusetts were loud in their promises to stand by their victim, and to sustain him in their common crime; but their guilty souls shrank from the necessary action. The brave and patriotic citizen soldiers of Vermont flung back their contempt upon the treasonable missive of their Governor, who was representing, not his State, but British feelings and interests, and remained to cover themselves with glory in one of the most brilliant achievements of the war. All honor to the memory of those gallant and true men! They were fit representatives of the heroes of Bennington.

In May, 1813, Governor Strong sent a message to the Legislature of Massachusetts in which he reviewed all the grounds for the declaration of war by our Government against England; and argued each one in favor of our enemy; and concluded by charging the Government of the United States with having prostituted itself to subserve the purposes and ambition of Bonaparte. A committee of both Houses responded, echoing the sentiments of the Governor, and denounced the war as improper, unjust, and impolitic on the part of the United States, and asserted that—

"While the oppressed nations of Europe are making a magnanimous and generous effort against the *common enemy* of free States, we alone, the *descendants of the Pilgrims*, sworn foe to civil and religious slavery, co-operate with the oppressor to bind nations in his chains and divert the forces of one of his enemies from the mighty conflict. Were not the territories of the United States sufficiently extensive before the *annexation of Louisiana*, the projected reduction of Canada, and the seizure of West Florida? Already have we witnessed the admission of a State beyond the territorial limits of the United States, peopled by inhabitants whose habits, language, religion, and laws are repugnant to the genius of our Government, in violation of the rights and interests of some of the parties to our national politics. The hardy people of the North stood in no need of the aid of the South to protect them in their liberties."

Such was the *loyalty* of Massachusetts to the United States in that dark and trying hour.

Josiah Quincy offered in the Senate of Massachusetts this preamble and resolution:

"Whereas a proposition has been made to this Senate for the adoption of sundry resolutions expressive of their sense of the gallantry and good conduct exhibited by Captain James Lawrence, commander of the United States ship-of-war Hornet, and the officers and crew of that ship, in the destruction of his Majesty's ship-of-war Peacock; and whereas it has been found that *former resolutions of this kind* passed on *similar occasions* relative to *other officers* engaged in a *like service* have given *great discontent* to many of the *good* people of this Commonwealth, it being considered by them as an encouragement and excitement to the continuance of the present *unjust, unnecessary*, and *iniquitous war*, and on that *account* the Senate of Massachusetts have deemed it their duty to *refrain from acting* on the said propositions; and whereas, also, this determination of the Senate may, without explanation, be construed into an intentional slight of Captain Lawrence, and denial of his particular merits, the Senate therefore deem it their duty to declare that they have a high sense of the naval skill and military and civil virtues of Captain James Lawrence, and that they have been withheld on said proposition *solely* from considerations relative to the *nature* and *principles of the present war*. And to the end that all misrepresentations on this subject may be obviated:

26

"*Resolved*, (as the sense of the Senate,) That in a war like the present, waged *without justifiable cause*, and prosecuted in a manner that indicates that *conquest and ambition are its real motives*. It is not becoming a *moral and religious people* to express any approbation of military or naval exploits which are not immediately connected with the defence of our sea-coast and soil."

This resolution was adopted by the Senate of Massachusetts 15th June, 1813. If the present Senators from that State had been there, they would have voted for it; and if any Senator had introduced one in the same terms in relation to any of our heroes who have fallen in this war, they would have voted the expulsion of such Senator.

The British authorities claimed that many prisoners taken by their cruizers on board American ships, as well native-born as naturalized citizens, were the subjects of their king; and they were thrown into loathsome prisons for safekeeping, to be tried and hung, or shot, as traitors to George III. In retaliation, and to insure the safety of our unfortunate captive countrymen, a United States marshal lodged some English prisoners in the jail of Worcester, Massachusetts, she and most of the States having, soon after the Constitution went into operation, passed a law granting the use of her jails to the United States Government. A mob of Massachusetts traitors and British sympathizers attacked the Worcester jail in force, broke it open, and set free the British hostages. The Worcester Gazette applauded this act of treasonable violence, and denounced the United States marshal as "a *lynx-eyed, full-blooded bloodhound* of Mr. Madison." The Boston Advertiser exulted over the success of this *infamous enterprise*, and denominated the liberated English prisoners as "gallant officers whom Mr. Madison desired to answer for the lives of *self-acknowledged traitors, victims of a barbarous and cruel policy.*"

Soon afterwards, the Legislature of Massachusetts, in consummation of the shame and crime of this affair, passed a law prohibiting the use of her jails to the United States even for the confinement of enemy prisoners to be held for the safety of our captive countrymen about to be executed by British authorities on fabricated charges of treason, &c. And that law authorized and required the keepers of all Massachusetts jails within thirty days from its passage to discharge any British prisoners that were confined in them.

At the gloomiest periods of the war, and when our country was most sorely pressed by her powerful foe, the Massachusetts traders and shippers took out licenses from the British consuls to carry supplies to her armies in Spain and Portugal, where they were held from augmenting the armies operating against us in their great struggle with Bonaparte; and her people also smuggled on a large scale to furnish the English armies and fleets acting against us on this continent and its coasts. One of those licensed ships was captured by an American cruiser while on her illicit voyage to Spain; and her owners had the assurance, to be sure many years afterwards, to offer a petition to Congress to be paid by the United States for their ship and cargo.

The ground upon which the British party in Massachusetts urged the original thirteen States to abandon their Government and the other States, and also upon which it proposed and pressed the project that New England should make a separate treaty of peace with Great Britain was, that they were *opposed* to the *war*, and *it was fatal to their interests*. But what language can express adequate contempt for their purpose to skulk back into the Union when the war should have terminated? They themselves furnished the only parallel, and that was in hanging out blue-lights to instruct and lead the public enemy to their country's disaster. That scheme, the separate treaty, was strenuously advocated by the Boston Advertiser.

An embargo law was passed as one of the war measures of the United States; but it was denounced by the traitors of Massachusetts as void and of no effect; and by connivance between them and the British consuls, was so extensively evaded and defeated as to produce but small results.

That party and its presses habitually disparaged and sneered at the victories won by our armies over their English enemies.

After the battle of the Thames, the Salem Gazette announced:

"At length the handful of British troops, which for more than a year have baffled the numerous armies of the United States in the invasion of Canada, deprived of the *genius* of the *immortal Brock*, have been obliged to yield to superior power and numbers."

The Boston Advertiser published of that battle:

"We shall surrender all our conquests at a peace. It is indeed a hopeful exploit for Harrison, with five thousand troops, who have been assembling and preparing ever since July, 1812, to fight and conquer four hundred and fifty worn-out, exhausted British regulars, whom the Indians had previously deserted."

Another journal of the same class pronounced Harrison's victory to be "the triumph of a crowd of *Kentucky savages* over a handful of brave men—no more than a march and their capture without fighting."

Here, sir, is a most flagitious violation of the truth in relation to the force of the British in that battle. They were five times as much as these papers state them to have been.

The gallant Lawrence fell, in the unequal fight of the Chesapeake with the Shannon, on his bloody quarter-deck, and his last words, "Don't give up the ship," became the ocean slogan of America.

Another of our naval captains, Crowninshield, under a flag of truce, sailed for Halifax to bring to Salem the remains of Lawrence, and while he was on this sacred mission, and all the true men of the nation were mourning the untimely death of the hero, and Story had been appointed to speak his funeral oration, one Boston journal announced that this solemn errand had been undertaken "by the *privateering captain, Crowninshield;* and the Boston Advertiser asked with scoffing malevolence, "What honor can be paid where a Crowninshield is chief mourner, and a Story chief priest? Governor Strong and his council, and most of the British party, had no honors or respect to pay to the martyrs in the cause of their country's rights and independence, and therefore they stayed away from the funeral of Lawrence.

Two years and six months of war brought peace to our country, and notwithstanding Massachusetts had struck in her cause with feeble arm and traitor's heart, yet the nation's prowess on land and ocean won for her *tacitly* but *forever* the great international rights for which she had unsheathed the sword.

Under the stimulants of fishing bounties and high protective tariffs, Massachusetts industry and enterprise soon commenced greatly to prosper. She regarded with sullen but not very vociferous disapprobation the acquisition of Florida. She probably would have been more demonstrative if the negotiator had not been her own Adams. When Texas was about to be annexed she became very eruptive, and not only reprobated the acquisition of foreign territory by joint resolution of Congress, but reiterated her ancient and uniform position, that it could not be legitimately done by the treaty-making power of our Government. Her Legislature passed these resolutions:

"*Resolved,* That there has hitherto been no precedent of the admission of foreign territory into the Union by legislation, and as the powers of legislation granted in the Constitution of the United States to Congress do not embrace the case of the admission of a foreign State or foreign territory by legislation into the Union, such an act of admission would have no binding force whatever upon the people of Massachusetts "

"*Resolved,* That the power never having been granted by the people of Massachusetts to admit into the Union States and Territories not within the same when the Constitution was adopted, *remains with the people,* and can only be exercised in such manner as the people *hereafter* shall designate and appoint."

It being the deliberate and oft-repeated judgment of Massachusetts that the United States Government had no power to acquire Louisiana, Florida, and Texas, and that their acquisition was detrimental to some of the States, and particularly to Massachusetts, and she having been to so recent a period vociferous and even frantic in the expression of her desire and purpose that the free States should cut loose from slavery and the slave States, one would have thought that she would have rushed to the acceptance of secession by the rebel States. Except a few crazy fanatics her people had always conceded fully that the Constitution and the Union protected slavery in the slave States. Mr. Webster, and all her eminent jurists and statesmen, except John Q. Adams, admitted the truth of that proposition, without any qualification or restriction whatever, and it was because there was no other escape from the protection which the Union and the Constitution gave to slavery that they were both to be repudiated by the abolitionists.

But the abolition party within a few years had got possession of the government of Massachusetts; and an extreme anti-slavery party, at the presidential election of 1856, had manifested a most rapid and extraordinary growth. Here was a new prospect breaking upon her radicals. They were not only meddling and fanatical, they not only loved money, but also power. She had always dominated and hectored over New England, and now opportunity was coming when, by alertness, daring, and decision, she could throw herself at the head of the great new movement, and assume in the nation and its councils the position and controlling influence which she had maintained in New England from the beginning. She would become the leading State of the United States; and above all, she could minister to hollow philanthropy, fierce fanaticism, and insatiable avarice, by procuring the slaves and lands of the rebels to be confiscated, and appropriating to herself the lion's share. She has entered upon this bold, ambitious, and wicked enterprise, driven on by the combined motive-power of all her leading characteristics, each one being highly stimulated by it.

28

A strong ingredient with the Massachusetts men also is this sentiment: "I have no slave; there is none who call me master; and in that respect no one shall be above me, and I'll bring all to my level." Never were there truer representatives of that sentiment than her two Senators. Never were there more unworthy and unsafe lights for a great people than they and those whom they represent.

In the excess of their hostility to slavery and slaveowners, I am at a loss to decide which dominates, the madman or the fiend. They show all the infernal malice of the one and the uncontrollable fury of the other. The English language has hardly any term of reproach and obloquy that they have not each, again and again, hurled at slavery and slaveowners. "The pollution of slavery," "the great sin of mankind," "the shame and disgrace of the age," "the foulest stain on Christendom," "the degrading effects of slavery," "the demoralizing influences of slavery," "the brutalizing influences of slavery," "the deformities and degradation of character produced by slavery," "slave-aristocracy," "slave oligarchy," "slave mongers," "slave-hunters," "slave-catchers," "slave-breeders," "slave-stealers," and "slave-pirates," are some of the epithets most prodigally used by those Senators in debate in this Chamber.

Sir, since the beginning of the present generation a new disease has sprung up in the United States. It is sometimes called "nigger on the brain," and I have never known two subjects that had it in a greater degree of violence than the two Senators from Massachusetts. The negro has made these two Senators. The worship of the negro and their demagoging in relation to him have given them public position and office, and brought them to the Senate of the United States. They have made the negro a hobby. Both have jumped astride of him, and it is impossible to determine which one is before and which one is behind. I believe they alternate their positions in that respect. But, sir, they fulfill the Scripture in one point. We are commanded to remember our creator in the days of our youth. The negro has created those two Senators; and from their youth to the present time they have been worshiping him with an eastern devotion, and they will continue this idolatry to the end of their lives. If they were to cease it Othello's occupation would be gone.

Let me read one or two passages from the speeches of the Senator from Massachusetts [Mr. SUMNER] in relation to the negro and a dissolution of the Union. In a speech delivered at Faneuil Hall, November 2, 1855, the Senator used these words:

"Not that I love the Union less but freedom more do I now in pleading this great case insist that freedom at all hazards shall be preserved. God forbid that for the sake of the Union we should sacrifice the very thing for which the Union was made."

What is his position? That the Union was made for negro freedom? Well, sir, it was a long day coming. The Union was first made in 1774, when the old Articles of Confederation were formed. Independence was declared in 1776, and the present Constitution was framed in 1787, all for the white man, and the negro was never known or dreamed of in any of those great transactions; and yet the honorable Senator says that the Union was made for the freedom of the negro!

On the 19th and 20th of May, 1856, in a speech delivered in the Senate, that Senator held this revolutionary language:

"Already the muster has begun. The strife is no longer local, but national. Even now while I speak, portents hang on all the arches of the horizon, threatening to darken the broad land, which already yawns with the mutterings of civil war. The fury of the propagandists of slavery and the calm determination of their opponents are now diffused from the distant Territory over widespread communities, and the whole country in all its extent—marshaling hostile divisions, and foreshadowing a strife, which, unless happily averted by the triumph of freedom, will become war.—fratricidal, parricidal war—with an accumulated wickedness beyond the wickedness of any war in human annals."

The gentleman's words were prophecy. They are in terrible course of execution; and he has given all the agency and energy to this war and revolution for the dissolution of the Union to put down slavery that he could command.

I will read one other passage from a speech by that Senator. In a debate in the Senate, June 26, 1854, Mr. Butler, of South Carolina, asked that Senator this question:

I would like to ask the Senator, if Congress repealed the fugitive slave law, would Massachusetts execute the constitutional requirements, and send back to the south the absconding slaves?
"Mr. SUMNER. Do you ask if I would send back slaves?
"Mr. BUTLER. Why, yes.
"Mr. SUMNER. Is thy servant a dog that he should do this thing?
"Mr. BUTLER. Then you would not obey the Constitution Sir, standing here before this tribunal, where you swore to support it, you rise and tell me that you regard it the office of a dog to support it. You stand in my presence, a coequal Senator, and tell me it is a dog's office to execute the Constitution of the United States
"Mr. SUMNER. I recognize no such obligation."

What obligation? No obligation to support the Constitution of the United States as it relates to the rendition of fugitive slaves. What exempted that Senator from that obligation? Had he not taken an oath to support the Constitution as a totality? What right had he to make any mental reservation? What right had he to except the fugitive slave law, or a provision of the Constitution which every man who swears to support it swears to sustain, to render back fugitive slaves? Sir, if a violation of the oath, taken in the broad terms in which the Senator has always taken it when he qualified as a member of this body, had been by law made perjury, and the Senator had violated that oath, as he has violated it so often, and he had been arraigned on the charge of perjury before any enlightened and independent court, what would have been the judgment?

Now, sir, I will proceed a little with the other Senator from Massachusetts, [Mr. WILSON.] They are par nobile fratrum. I do not know, according to their ideas, which is the grandest and greatest. According to my own I do not know which is least, which is most false to the Constitution and to the loyalty that is justly due to their Government and to the Constitution and Union of these States. They come in here and make an exhibit of this almost daily that is abhorrent to every man who has any moral principle.

But, sir, the other Senator from Massachusetts, the chairman of the Committee on Military Affairs, the representative of war, "horrid war," in the Senate, declared in a speech at Syracuse, New York, October 29, 1859:

"I tell you, fellow-citizens, the Harper's Ferry outbreak was the legitimate consequence of the teachings of the Republican party."

Sir, that is the truth, and it is a lesson which the Senator sought to inculcate; which every traitor who meditated the dissolution of the Union and the deprivation of the slave-owners of the South of the protection and guarantee which that instrument gave to their property—it was a lesson leading to an act which they all meditated. Sir, what can we think of a man who so boldly and defiantly announces it? There was a murderous and treasonable raid by John Brown upon the Commonwealth of Virginia, carrying blood and violence and treason and crime into a peaceful community, far distant from his residence; and the Senator avows that this act was the legitimate result of the teachings, as every body knows that it was, of the Republican party.

Mr. WILSON. Will the Senator allow me a word?

Mr. DAVIS. I prefer you to wait until I get through.

Mr. WILSON. I wish simply to say that the records of the Senate show that that statement is not correct. I never made any such assertion. Mr. Hunter once brought it up in the Senate, and I referred to the speech which I actually made, in which I stated precisely the opposite doctrine.

Mr. DAVIS. I accept the Senator's explanation. I withdraw that charge; but I will bring up another, and see what answer he will make to that.

On the 20th day of November, 1859—

"A large and enthusiastic meeting of the citizens of this town [Natick, Massachusetts] was called to consider the following resolutions:
"Whereas resistance to tyrants is obedience to God; Therefore,
"Resolved, That it is the highest duty of the slaves to resist their masters; and it is the right and duty of the people of the North to incite slaves to resistance and aid them in it."

My information is that that Senator was present at this meeting when this resolution passed, and that it passed nemine contradicente, and the Senator's voice was not raised in remonstrance against the atrocity of the sentiment expressed in that resolution.

Mr. WILSON. Does the Senator wish an explanation now?

Mr. DAVIS. Is it any denial?

Mr. WILSON. I have to say simply this: that was a meeting called by some anti-slavery men whom we denominate in our country as the "Garrison abolitionists." Some seven or eight hundred persons went to the meeting as lookers-on, and did not vote on that resolution, or take any part in it. Probably not over seven or eight men voted on that resolution, or had any part in it. Not one in twenty of those who were present had any sympathy with the meeting; but it was a meeting called by other persons, and they did not wish to interfere with it. My own views were fully expressed at the time in a letter denying any sympathy with it whatever, and in condemnation of it.

Mr. DAVIS. I accept the Senator's explanation; but I think he was at a very improper place, and in very bad company. [Laughter.]

Now, Mr. President, I will say one word as to negro insurrections, and in relation to the policy of the Government in arming and organizing negro soldiers. I have some knowledge of negro nature. I have studied it from my infancy. I know of no people that have kinder or more benevolent feelings toward a race whom they deem to be their inferiors than have the slaveholders of Kentucky toward their slaves. I know of no slaveholder who would not imperil his life if it were necessary to defend his slave from wrong and violence. If to support this war in its just and proper conduct in the proper mode of carrying it on, slavery had fallen as a necessary consequence, I know of no man in the State of Kentucky who is for the Union that would have made any complaint. It would have presented itself to them in this aspect: here is an alternative, the preservation of the Union or the overthrow of slavery ; and my colleague of the other House, who owns about two hundred slaves, and every slaveholder in the State who is a Union man, would have yielded his slaves just as he would any of his other property, to the exigencies of the war and to the just demands of the Government in carrying it on. All that we asked was that slaves should share the fate of other property in this war; that the war should not be carried on for their defense nor for the destruction of the institution. We believed that all policy to make slaves a component part of the Army would result disastrously to the Government and to the country, and I have no doubt whatever that this has proved true. But we protested and will continue to protest against making war upon the property of loyal people.

Mr. President, I know the nature of slaves, of that population. There have been contemplated slave insurrections in Virginia; some in the State of Kentucky. We all know the extent of the outrages that ensued in the insurrection of the slaves of San Domingo. There is a general law in relation to the white and black races; the black race desires the white race; and whenever there is an insurrection consummated, or suppressed in its embryo, the leaders of the insurrection generally select in anticipation for themselves the handsomest and most attractive white women for their wives. That is a law of the race; and wherever there is an extensive insurrection, and violence and passion and lust obtain the ascendant, the outrageous enormities that are and will be perpetrated by the black race are fearful and too horrid to narrate. Nevertheless, I will recite one that occurred on the Bayou Teche in western Louisiana.

It was communicated to me by a citizen of one of the parishes on that bayou, a Mr. Carlin, a Spanish creole, a loyal man, a gentleman, a man of intelligence, and of as true integrity to the Government and the Union as there is in it. He had a son who had reached the years of manhood. He urged the noble and educated youth to take a position in the Army as a private, that he might learn the art of war and acquire the capacity for subordinate command. The young man did so. He served out his time, and at the end his father procured him a second lieutenancy. He returned to Virginia to join his regiment and assume his command; but before he reached their rendezvous they had left for Gettysburg. He followed on, and reached Gettysburg during the protracted conflict. He shouldered his musket, took his position as a private in the ranks, and there poured out his young life, it and all the bright hopes of a fond father were offered there upon the altar of his country.

His father narrated to me this fact. There was a Mr. Bossiere, a creole planter on the Bayou Teche, a man of wealth, of education, and of refinement. He was aged, was paralytic, and helpless. The march of armies drove from his neighborhood all his friends, leaving him and his motherless daughter exposed and unprotected. A negro soldier wearing the uniform of the United States came to this defenseless house, and there, in the presence of the powerless father, violated the person of his daughter.

Sir, that is one only of the many and untold and most horrid incidents that have no doubt characterized this war. Shame and ruin, mute despair, and blasted hopes of happiness have silenced the voice forever of most of the victims of such diabolical lust. Mr. President, could there be a stronger case than this appealing to manhood—man the natural protector of woman—to turn from the policy that brings such heartrending enormities? But, sir, such instances as these would be brought up in vain to cause to relent the fanatical, fierce, frenzied and perverted hearts and souls of the Senators from Massachusetts. At such recitations they would turn with the sardonic smile of fiends from the white woman's direst woe, from the ruin of all that is innocent and lovely in the most cultivated and attractive of the sex of the white race.

Already it is said that the white population in some of the southern States where the negroes have been enlisted are fleeing to places of concealment and safety. The negroes know these hiding-places, and the secret ways and paths to them, and they

31

are organized into the Army, and it is boasted that they are already upon the hunt of their victims. I can fancy the Senator from Massachusetts [Mr. Wilson] in a position where he would feel something of the pride and the glory and honor of war according to the scale and dignity of his courage and great soul. It would be as Colonel of one of those black regiments, those fiends inflamed by infernal passions, and leading them on to hunt out, to murder, or to bring to a fate more horrible than murder, these fleeing and helpless women and children.

But, sir, I have something more to say to that Senator. When I took my seat in this body I found him always the most forward and most reckless assailant of property in negroes. According to his judgment, I had the audacity to remonstrate against a series of systematic measures which he introduced to assail and destroy that property. I did this because of the great interests of my constituents in it, and because of the foul injustice and iniquity of the policy generally. I never could say a word by way of remonstrance, argument, reason, or expostulation against those measures without receiving the coarse and the insulting rebuke of that Senator.

I recollect on one occasion he called me to order for speaking treasonable words, as he assumed. He was required by the occupant of the chair to reduce the words to writing. He recited them—I do not recollect whether he reduced them to writing or not—but I pronounced the words as he reduced them to writing, or stated them, to be untrue and false in fact. He called upon the reporter. The reporter read his report of my words, and it corroborated my version and contradicted that of the Senator, and then the matter dropped.

Sir, the Senator has been a sort of general whipper-in, not only of the Black Republican party, but of the whole Senate. He has assumed to rebuke, to chide, to domineer, to bully Senators at his pleasure, without much regard to their political position. Sir, I think there ought to be inscribed on his most impudent front the words, "The self-constituted gagger of the Senate."

Mr. WILSON. I call the Senator to order.

Mr. DAVIS resumed:

On the 5th of January I submitted to the senate a series of resolutions chiefly condemnatory of the abuses and usurpations of power by the Executive of the United States. The member from Massachusetts, on the 8th, moved a resolution for my expulsion from the Senate, basing it on the 13th one of my series, which came up for consideration on the 31th. That Senator opened the debate by reading a speech in support of his resolution. I do not know who wrote the speech for him, but the Senate will bear me witness he read it very badly. It was replete with gross personalities and vulgar ribaldry, some specimens of which I will read. "Having," says that member, "a reasonable degree of confidence in my own powers of endurance, I entered upon the task of reading these resolves aimed at the President of the United States, the members of his Cabinet, the majority of these Chambers, the laws of Congress, the proclamations and orders of the Commander-in-chief of our army, and of all who are clothed with authority to administer the Government of the United States. I groped through the mass of vituperative accusations with mingled emotions of indignation and pity."

"In this farrago of spleen and malice, the Chief Magistrate, his associates and supporters, struggling to preserve the life of the nation, are accused, arrayed, and condemned."

The Senator must not trifle here. He must recollect that he is in the Senate of the United States, and not at a barbecue in Kentucky. Senators cannot fail here to comprehend the import and meaning of the words and phrases introduced in these resolutions, and they know that these are not the words and phrases of statesmen, but of babbling fools."

These are a few specimens of the spirit and scurrilous language in which the member from Massachusetts opened his attack upon me. I replied at considerable length, not only endeavoring to defend myself, but to carry the war into Africa. The Senator rejoined, and after this manner:

"Mr. President: It is not my purpose to notice in detail the illogical, rambling, and incoherent utterances that the Senate has been forced to listen to for near three hours. Seldom has the Senate of the United States been compelled to listen to such a farrago of *brutality, indecency, treason and falsehood.*" "He (the Senator from Kentucky) rises here in the Senate of the United States, flippantly speaks of States and public men, bringing against States and public men false and vituperative accusations, on authority of what he has heard and what he has been informed, swift to accuse, fierce, bitter, and unrelenting in denunciation, reckless alike of facts that should govern *honorable* men," &c.

He then proceeds to charge me with having violated the *proprieties that govern honorable men and gentlemen.* What does that member know of these proprieties?

When did he ever practice them! He speaketh of things of which he knoweth nothing.

In my reply to that member I alluded to the fact that on the day of the first battle of Bull Run he was applied to by the father of a gallant young soldier, who had fallen mortally wounded, to aid him to get the son off the field, and that he declined to render any assistance. In his rejoinder the Senator from Massachusetts turned to me and asked this question: "Did the Senator manufacture that libelous accusation?" I answered, "It was told me by a soldier." He added: "The Senator was told so. Sir, whoever told the Senator so told him an unmitigated and unqualified lie, that had not a semblance or shadow of truth in it."

Sir, the soldier who related that incident to me was Major McCook, deceased, late a paymaster in the service of the United States, and the father of General Alexander McCook and brothers, all of them having joined the army, and two having fallen in the service. I am informed, on good authority, that he communicated the same fact to several gentlemen in this city when he brought back the remains of his son. Will the member from Massachusetts, in the presence of the Senate, deny that he knew on the day, and after the repulse of our army that young McCook was lying dangerously wounded near Centerville, or somewhere between the battlefield and the fortifications around Washington City? Will he deny that he saw McCook, the father, on that day? Will he deny that that father requested him to give assistance in getting his son into an ambulance or some other conveyance, and that he declined, saying that he "had a wife and children to care for," or words to that effect? Whatever that Senator may answer to those special interrogatories, Major McCook stated the fact to me, and I have no doubt to many others, not in confidence, but publicly, and in terms of reproach to the member from Massachusetts. That soldier and father is now in his grave, but when living his life was illustrated by spotless truth and honor, and his statement of any fact could not be shaken by any denial or asseveration of the living Senator from Massachusetts.*

The word of that Senator stands discredited in the public journals of the country. In March, 1862, he entered into a debate in the Senate, in which he took ground in favor of discontinuing further recruiting, and for the discharge of 150,000 soldiers from the army. The New York Herald published a summary of his remarks at the time. Some months afterwards that Senator made a speech at Newton, in which he was reported to have said in reference to this synopsis of his speech in the Senate: "There is not only no truth, but there is not a shadow of truth on which to to lay the foundation of the assertion." "I have always maintained that Government wanted more men. So much, Mr. Chairman, in explanation of the false position which the New York Herald has sought to place me in, and which other papers have echoed." These two denials of the Senator are very similar, and equally positive; but as to the latter the Herald nails that Senator to the counter, by quoting from his speech these words:

Mr. Wilson, of Massachusetts—*The Senator from Maine the other day proposed to reduce the number of men authorized by law down to five hundred thousand. I agree with him in that. Still we have not been able to do it. It was suggested also that we ought to stop recruiting. I agree to that. I have over and over again been to the War Office and urged upon the department to stop recruiting in every part of the country. We have had the promise that it should be done, yet every day, in different parts of the country, we have accounts of men being raised and brought forth to fill up the ranks of regiments. The papers tell us that in Tennessee and other parts of the country where our armies move, we are filling up the ranks of the army. I believe we have to-day one hundred and fifty thousand more men under the pay of the Government than we need or can well use. I have not a doubt of it; and I think it ought to be checked. I think the War Department ought to issue peremptory orders forbidding the enlistment of another soldier into the volunteer force of the United States until the time shall come when we need them. We can obtain them any time when we need them.* —Washington Globe, March 29, 1862, part 2, page 1,417.

*A gentleman of the highest character for truth, integrity, and honor, has given me this information. He went out from Washington to the neighborhood of Bull Run on the day of the first battle. In the vicinity of Centerville he came upon Major McCook, now deceased, who informed him that his son, a youth, had been overtaken by some rebel cavalry in an adjoining field, who required him to surrender, and he answering that he would not, they had fired at and wounded him; and he had gotten him over the fence into the road. That Senator Wilson, of Massachusetts, had just passed along, and being requested by him to assist him to get his son into a house near by that he might be cared for. This he refused, saying that he had a wife and children, and must take care of himself, and hurried on but was still in view. McCook spoke of the matter with a good deal of feeling against Wilson. This gentleman then helped McCook to place his son in the house, and afterwards into a wagon, which started for Washington, but before it reached its destination he died. The name of this gentleman is Dr. J. J. Jones, of Louisiana, at present sojourning in this city. I have seen no one who has been able to inform me, whether the time of the member from Massachusetts, when he hurried away from the dying young soldier for Washington, was equal to "Flora Temple's" best.

But I concede I was misinformed, and erred in my reply to the Senator, as to the order of some facts in his military career, which it is very important should be correctly recorded in history. He informs us, and no doubt truly, that it was not *before*, but *after* the first battle of Bull Run, that he raised a regiment in Massachusetts. That his earliest visit to the field was some two days after the battle of Blackburn's Ford, and very shortly before the battle of Bull Run, and close by. He had heard that some Massachusetts soldiers had been wounded, and repaired to their camp to nurse them. A very praiseworthy object, and it being impossible to suppose that he had less fitness for it than his present engagements, he should have continued to nurse the soldiers. He does not deny that after he had raised his regiment a grand pageant was got up on Boston common, in honor of it and himself; and to stimulate his warlike ardor, a very eloquent and stirring address was made to him by one of the most accomplished orators, not only of Boston, but America. He no doubt struggled and swelled to mate himself in his reply to the grandeur of the occasion, and the eloquence of the other speaker. We have all heard how the celebrated Capt. Bobadil proposed to use up with a few men a very large opposing army. I suppose that his work was tame and slow compared with the rapid and wholesale destruction with which the hero of Natick proclamated to overwhelm all rebeldom. Near the close of his third speech against me, the Senator brought into this Chamber "Canterbury Hall," and spoke of the introduction of a *farce* upon its boards. Now, I suggest to the Senator, that if he will advertise for the particular evening when he will present himself on the Canterbury's boards, to recite his Boston common's war speech, and will belt himself again to that long sword, and take a few preliminary turns on the front part of the stage, with his martial strut of eighteen inches a pace, accompanied by his peculiar hitch and jerk, and will then give his reading of the speech, suiting the action to the word, according to his own conception, he will have not only the largest audience, but will produce the baldest and flatest farce that has ever yet signalized Canterbury, or any other boards.

The *neophite Colonel* started from Boston for the seat of war by this city, with the most redundant stock of courage that warrior ever took aboard; but it ebbed in a geometrical ratio as he approximated the enemy, and even before he reached Washington, the last vestage of it was gone. He had been close to the battle of Bull Run, and the breeze had then wafted to his olfactories the odor of "villianous saltpetre." He had heard the thunders of battle and seen its murky incense offered up to Mars. When he got near to its scene, instinctive dread came over him, and it was reproduced to his memory and imagination like a terrible apparition. I heard a member of the other House, from South Carolina, announce in stentorian voice that he was born a stranger to fear; one of his colleagues immediately said to me, "I was not born exactly there, but in that neighborhood." The member from Massachusetts was born far away from both *localities*, and had no stomach to go back to Bull Run again. He consequently doffed his sword and eagles, but had none of the fussy pomp with which he had assumed them; and when, or how, or where they became separated, no one but a few of the initiated ever knew.

Throughout his three speeches against me, the member from Massachusetts made constant proffer of himself as a born and practiced scavenger. In the third one he compared me to a fractious little wife who very much berated her husband, and on its being brought to his attention, he remarked, it seemed to do the little thing a great deal of good, but himself no hurt. He would never be suspected of being that husband, in whose conduct there was a forbearance and decorum that he could never be supposed to be able to approach. In his rejoinder to my reply, he characterized it as "the twitterings of a cock snowbird." That member had never been associated in my mind with the idea of a bird; if the fact had been otherwise, it would doubtless have been some most unclean bird. But I will tell him what did come up spontaneously in my mind when I looked upon him. It was "Jeremiah Leathers," alias "Jeremiah Colbath," alias "Henry Wilson." He denounced me as "pro-slavery drunk," intimated that I was frightened by his resolution for my expulsion, and alluded to my "courage oozing out of my fingers' ends;" and also that it was with me as with Falstaff, "discretion being the better part of valor." I think that member must himself be about convinced that he has neither *valor* nor *discretion*. It has been said that Bob Acres' courage oozed out of his fingers' ends. The Senator denied that he *run* from the battle of Bull Run, admitted that he walked several miles, and says he was then taken up by a friend in his buggy. I have no doubt that in that three or four miles he did the *tallest walking* and made the best time of the war; and that what courage he had had previously, oozed out at some other place than his fingers' ends; and when he crossed the Potomac, he was a fitter sub-

2

ject to be laved in that river than was the dirty soldier of the Peninsula in the Gaudiana.

He dared me to read my series of resolutions at the head of any regiment in the army, and said if I attempted it I would be hung on the highest tree. Well, I will make this proposition to the Senator. Let him get from his master at the White House, an order that he, or any other, or as many other of their champions as they may select, and I, shall have safe conduct to all our armies, and the soldiers shall have perfect liberty to listen to a discussion of those resolutions by us, and to form their free and independent judgment and action upon them, and I will risk the hanging. I have confidence in the citizen soldiery of the United States, in their devotion to the Constitution and the rights and liberties which it guaranties to them. The member pronounces a foul libel upon them when he says, that if I were to appear before them to plead that great cause, of myself, of them, of our countrymen, and of mankind, that they would murder me for attempting to bear an humble part in the great work of their restoration.

But whilst the mind of the member is running upon hazzardous undertakings, I will make this proposition to him: let him go to Kentucky, and there set up his negro-stealing operations, denounce the fugitive slave laws of Congress in the gross and treasonable language which he so often uses in this Chamber, and organize and machinate to defeat their execution, as he has long been doing in Massachusetts, and what fate would await him? He would be consigned to the penitentiary and put to work in a cobbler's stall. His crimes would make him infamous The labor would be only to fill up his time and to mitigate his punishment by diverting his thoughts from the unbroken contemplation of the guilt of his soul. The people of Kentucky honor labor and laborers. That class, in every country, constitute mainly its physical and moral strength, and its greatest glory. A laborer of plain good sense, morals and principles, of proper sensibilities and deference to others, and of upright and decorous walk in life, is one of the truest of gentlemen, and there are millions of them among our countrymen. They are so estimated by all the people of Kentucky, and their regret is that a merciful administration of criminal justice requires that felons in their punishment should be allowed to dishonor labor.

As that Senator spoke his speech in this Chamber, he annunciated that nine tenths of the people of the loyal States, including Kentucky, would condemn my resolutions; but, in the Globe, he changed it to "an overwhelming majority." By what authority does he speak on this or any other point for the loyal States generally, and particularly for Kentucky? He has but one warrant, and that is his unequaled assurance. He is a most rapid census-taker on this subject, but I think it will turn out that he is yet more false.

In one of his three speeches there is this passage: "But the Senator from Kentucky reproaches Massachusetts for her legislation intended to protect her own citizens against the inhuman provisions of that fugitive slave law, whose provisions so gladden his heart and fill his capacious brain. The Senator mounts his desk and reads to the Senate that infamous enactment that has brought so much shame and dishonor upon our country in the face of the Christian and civilized world." So great is one of the infirmities of the member that he cannot relate truly an incident occurring in his own presence, and of the Senate. Being fatigued, I reclined on my desk. It was not *my desk*, but the Senator *himself* that I *mounted*.

His third speech appears in the Globe materially changed, and a good deal improved from what it was as he delivered it. Some superior workman to himself has certainly been pruning and polishing it down. He assumed that I had warped away from my resolutions, and then added: "I say with these modifications and denials, the resolutions become simply a farce, one that they would be ashamed to put upon the boards at *Canterbury Hall.* The whole country will launch its gibes and its jeers at them. They are nothing, and they mean nothing. 'Revolt does not mean revolt.' The taking of Government into your own hands does not mean it. Calling a National Convention to exercise this power does not mean anything only a pamphlet, and some *old hunker* nominated for President to be beaten. 'A subsidized army' is not a subsidized army. I do not know that the negro janazaries are to be denied. I suppose these colored troops stand as negro janazaries. But, sir, I accept all these disclaimers. I do not say that the Senator in drafting them was very brave, and that as he comes before the Senate and country with them his knees smote together, or that his courage oozed out of his fingers' ends; but certainly I think the Senator has taken Falstaff's advice, that 'discretion is the better part of valor.' The resolutions, as *I* say they mean nothing, are nothing, and become a mere farce, and *I* drop them and withdraw the resolution."

Mr. President, the member from Massachusetts is fortified by a cordon of impudence and mendacity that make him impregnable and unapproachable. He, him-self, fabricates *modifications, denials,* and *explanations* of my resolutions in general and indefinite terms, *falsely* imputes them *to me,* and declares that he *accepts* them, and then withdraws the resolution for my expulsion.,

I will read from the Congressional Globe what occurred in the Senate on the 8th January when the member from Massachusetts moved my expulsion:

"Mr. WILSON. Mr. President, I rise for the purpose of submitting a resolution of a personal nature. I find on my desk a series of resolutions introduced into the Senate on the 5th instant by the Senator from Kentucky, [Mr. DAVIS.] Those resolutions class the Government and its sup-porters——

"The VICE PRESIDENT. The Senator will first submit his resolution.

"Mr. WILSON Very well; I submit my resolution.

"The VICE PRESIDENT. The resolution will be read for the information of the Senate.

"The Secretary read the resolution, as follows:

"Whereas the Hon. GARRETT DAVIS, a Senator from the State of Kentucky, did on the 5th day of January, A. D. 1864, introduce into the Senate of the United States a series of resolutions in which, among other things, it is declared that 'the people North ought to revolt against their war leaders and take this great matter into their own hands,' thereby meaning to incite the people of the United States to revolt against the President of the United States and those in authority who support him in the prosecution of the war to preserve, protect, and defend the Constitution and the Union, and to take the prosecution of the war into their own hands: Therefore,

"*Be it resolved,* That the said GARRETT DAVIS has, by the introduction of the resolutions afore-said, been guilty of advising the people of the United States to treasonable, insurrectionary, and rebellious action against the Government of the United States, and of a gross violation of the privi-leges of the Senate; for which cause he is hereby expelled.

"The PRESIDING OFFICER, (Mr. ANTHONY in the chair.) Will the Senate give unanimous consent for the consideration of the resolution at the present time?'

"Mr. WILSON. I do not propose to call it up for action at the present time, but I intend to do so at some time hereafter, for I desire to record my vote upon it. I have offered this resolution without consultation with any Senator, on my own responsibility. Often I heard the men who or-ganized this treasonable rebellion threaten the dissolution of the Union, and make treasonable appeals to the country, and when this bloody revolution opened I resolved that if I ever heard in this ' hamber more treasonable utterances, I would move the expulsion of the Senator uttering words of treason. These are not words uttered in debate, but they are in the Senator's resolutions. He tells the people, he asks the Senate to tell the people of the country, the loyal men of the North and the rebels of the South, to revolt; yes, sir, to revolt against their war leaders, to take affairs into their own hands, to elect delegates to a national convention, to stop the war. No proposition was ever made in the Senate of the United States, not even by the conspirators who organized this slaveholder's rebellion, more unconstitutional, seditious, and rebellious. ' If the people follow his advice, if they revolt against the President, Congress, the Supreme Court, the ' war leaders,' if they take the power into their own hands, if they go into national convention, a convention unknown to the Constitution and the laws, assume authority to close the war, and adjust the terms of peace in defiance of the Government of the United States, war, civil war, is inevitable, and the loyal States will be plunged into the fire and blood of internal strife. Stripped of its verbiage, the Senator's proposition means this, nothing less.

"Mr. DAVIS. Mr. President, the resolution of the Senator from Massachusetts presents a gar-bled version of my resolution. It does not embody my resolution so as to express its sense; and the inferences that that Senator draws from it are not authorized by its language or its spirit. Sir, what did that honorable Senator admit within the last two years? He admitted that when his own State was in a state of rebellion against the United States, he sympathized with that rebellion.

"Mr. WILSON No, sir

"Mr. DAVIS. I think the Senator did. Mr. WILSON. No, sir.

"Mr. DAVIS. I interrogated that Senator and his colleague in relation to their course and sym-pathies in the Burns case that occurred in Boston some years ago. 'The galled jade winces;' 'my withers are unwrung.' When the gentleman speaks of treason and disloyalty to his Government, he speaks from the recesses of his own heart, not mine.

"He puts his own interpretation on the resolution that I offered. That resolution I abide by; but I deny that its authorizes the conclusion the Senator from Massachusetts is forcibly trying to deduce from it; far from it. It however strikes the Senator on this point: he is here an advocate for the interference of the military power at elections, to destroy their freedom, and to appoint to office by the bayonet instead of the free suffrages of the people. Now, my resolution—its purport, its meaning, its spirit—is, that the people shall rise at the polls and take the power of this Govern-ment and of this country, that properly belongs to them, there. at that constitutional forum, into their own hands, by peaceful convention; that the people North and the people South shall both do it, and repudiate their war leaders—leaders who desire a continuance of this terrible struggle, and who are opposed to its peaceful settlement. Sir, I give them that counsel there everywhere. The thought of mutiny or disaffection in the Army was not in my mind. How is it with the Senator? If I recollect aright, he stated that his sympathies were with Burns in the Massachusetts insurrection.

"Mr. WILSON. Never.

"Mr. DAVIS. Were you against his rescue?

"Mr WILSON. I had nothing to do with it; and had no knowledge of it until after it trans-pired. I was not in my own State at the time.

"Mr. DAVIS. Did you ever condemn that insurrection? Did you ever do anything to put it down—its spirit?

"Mr. WILSON. There was no occasion; it was put down quickly.

"Mr. DAVIS. Did you ever do or say anything to assert the authority of the laws and of the United States in that insurrection? Did you ever express any condemnation of it? No, sir; no.

"Mr. HARLAN. Mr. President, I rise to a question of order. I desire to know if there is any subject before the Senate.

"The PRESIDING OFFICER. There is no subject before the Senate. The Senator from Mas-sachusetts did not ask for the present consideration of his resolution.

"Mr. HARLAN. I move then that the Senate do now adjourn. ['Oh, no!']"

It is thus seen that at the moment when the resolution for my expulsion was sprung in the Senate by the member from Massachusetts, I charged him with garbling that resolution of my series on which he based his, and giving an unauthorized and false interpretation to mine. I protested that neither its language or spirit meant any appeal to violence, or any other remedy than a peaceable convention to be elected by the people of all the States, north and south.

On the 11th January, I called up the resolution of expulsion, and at my instance it was made the special order for the 13th.

On the 13th of January I again called up the resolution, when the Senator from Massachusetts read his opening speech. I replied, and he rejoined; and then the subject was postponed until the morrow. On the 18th of January I again called up the resolution, when it was referred by the Senate to the judiciary committee, which on the 25th reported it back, asking to be discharged from its consideration. Thereupon I moved to make it the special order for the morrow, when it came up. Mr. Howard (of Michigan) rose in its support. Before he proceeded, I asked his courtesy to permit the Secretary to read a note which I had addressed to the chairman of the judiciary committee, in these words:

"WASHINGTON CITY, *January* 20, 1864.

"SIR: I was taken wholly by surprise at the presentation of the resolution to expel me from the Senate. I had not expected, or even thought of the resolution which was made the ground of that proceeding, or any one, or the whole of the series producing any such movement. I therefore avowed, in substance, distinctly, that the mover of the resolution for my expulsion interpreted the resolution on which he based his erroneously and injuriously to me. That in offering those resolutions I had no purpose to invite the the Army to mutiny, or the people to sedition, or any violence whatever; but it was to exhort the whole people, North and South, to terminate the war by a constitutional settlement of their difficulties and reconstruction of the Union; and that the series of resolutions would not fairly admit of any other construction; all of which I now reaffirm.

"I am prompted to make this disavowal again, in this form, to place it upon the records of the Senate, it having as yet only appeared in the reports of its debates. And with this note, which I request you to lay before the committee, I submit the case on my part to its action.

"Yours, &c.,   GARRETT DAVIS.

"The CHAIRMAN *of the Committee on the Judiciary of the Senate.*

"Mr. HOWARD. Mr. President, the temper exhibited in the letter of the honorable member from Kentucky just read from the Chair seems to indicate certainly to my mind a regret that his resolutions have placed him in this unpleasant predicament; and I desire now to say to the Senator from Kentucky that, if such be the fact, and he desires leave to withdraw the resolutions which are the foundation of the resolution of the Senator from Massachusetts for his expulsion, I shall certainly be very happy to grant him the leave so far as I am concerned, and I presume that will be the universal sense of the Senate.

"Mr. DAVIS. The Senator from Michigan has paused, I suppose, that I may respond to his suggestion, (which being assented to by him) I added, having declared generally the meaning of those resolutions. I adhere to them. I will never withdraw them, never, never.

"Mr. HOWARD. Under the circumstances, sir, before proceeding with the remarks which I had intended to make upon this subject, I will offer an amendment to the resolution of the Senator from Massachusetts, which I now send to the Chair.

"The VICE PRESIDENT. The amendment will be read.

"The Chief Clerk read the amendment, which was to strike out of the resolution the word "expelled," and insert in lieu thereof the words "censured by the Senate."

"The VICE PRESIDENT. The question will be on agreeing to the amendment."

The Senator moved to substitute *censure* for *expulsion*, and made an elaborate speech.

I have exhibited all the *modifications, denials,* and *disclaimers* which I made, and which the member from Massachusetts says so far mollified him as to move him to withdraw his resolution of expulsion. It is shown that my modifications, *denials,* and *disclaimers* were simply a denunciation of him for having *garbled* my *resolution* and given it a *false* and *forced interpretation;* and a protest, that neither its *spirit* or *language* would authorize his conclusions; that the one on which he based his resolution of expulsion, or any, or all the series, did not invite to any mutiny of the army, sedition of the people, or other violent remedy for the public abuses and wrongs which I denounced. I disclaimed both the *fact* and the *intention* of recommending any remedy of violence and revolution, and avowed the potent and specific one, a national convention of all the States.

I assumed distinctly this ground, and the whole of it, at the moment when the Senator first launched his charge against me. If it was such a surrender by me, as he now claims it to be, why did he not accept it when it was made, and then ask to withdraw his resolution of expulsion? Why did he continue to press it, and permit it to remain before the Senate for twenty days longer, consuming its time and obstructing the public business? Two Senators [Mr. HOWARD of Michigan, and Mr. MORRILL of Maine] came to his assistance in the debate. Messrs. JOHNSON of Maryland, HALE of New Hampshire, LANE of Indiana, FESSENDEN of Maine, ANTHONY of Rhode Island, and FOSTER of Connecticut, in debate, opposed the movement against me. The Senator had boasted on the introduction of his resolution, that it was his own act, and without consultation with a single Senator. On the 27th January, the fact was revealed to him that in the demise of his resolution he would be nearly in as lean a minority as he was at its birth. It was then that the instinctive *magnanimity* of a *little, malignant* and *cowardly spirit* asserted its dominion over him, and he determined to withdraw it. He came into the Senate the next day with the deliberate and final purpose to withdraw it: he rose for that object; had the baseness to utter against me another of his scullionly speeches, and at its close did withdraw it. This was done with the unanimous concurrence of the Senate, the body being satisfied that the movement should never have been made. But that Senator, in the plenitude of his arrogance, seems almost unconscious that he had obtruded this matter upon the Senate, and thereby made it their business; and he treats it as his own personal affair, and the Senate as the machinery with which he was managing it according to his own will and pleasure. "*I accept* these disclaimers." "*I say*, then, they (my resolutions) *mean nothing, are nothing*, and *become a mere farce. I drop them and withdraw the resolution*." Brainless and impudent simpleton! to suppose that he was regarded or thought of in the matter at all, except so far as he was constantly obtruding himself upon the attention of the Senate. Had he been silent, he would soon have been forgotten.

But, as he had his third speech printed in the Congressional Globe, he dropped out of it "Canterbury Hall," and "some old hunker candidate for the presidency" he changed into "some respectable conservative." But that Senator having brought Canterbury Hall into this Chamber, he shall not give so summary and quiet an exit to it. I have heard of a great many respectable people, members of Congress, soldiers, strangers and citizens patronizing that theatre; and the most damaging fact against its respectability that had reached my ears, is, that the member from Massachusetts was one of its patrons. I have no doubt that curiosity and assurance propelled him occasionally into the boxes, but, from his reputation, that his distinctive tastes generally prompted him to seek more congenial company, of both sexes and colors, in the upper gallery. But were I to make a suggestion on this point to the managers of the Canterbury, it would be, that they improve the respectability of their establishment by excluding him from it wholly, pit, boxes, and galleries.

But my appeal to the body of the people of all the States, North and South, to meet in National Convention and stop this bloody and desolating war, and to re-establish the great principles of concession and compromise, and the powers, rights, liberties and privileges reserved to the people and States respectively, upon which Washington and his associates had based our blended system of National and State Governments, is what appals the member from Massachusetts. The thought of such a movement makes him rave like a mad dog in the presence of water. In his phrenzy he declares that the assembling of such a convention would be *treason*, horrid treason; and if it should attempt to exercise any powers belonging to the Government of the United States, it would be the duty of the President to *arrest!* to *imprison!* to *try!* to *convict!* to *condemn!* and *hang!* the *members of that convention for treason!* Blood and thunder! what a swelling climax of military justice, moving along in all its dread and stately steps, and the whole to be performed by one public functionary, and in punishment of the exercise of the undoubted right of the sovereign power of the country, the people of the United States, to perform the greatest and most beneficient act within the competency of mortals. The people of all the States, calling a convention to represent their unlimited political sovereignty and power, and one of the most base and puny of presidential tools hurling against it such senseless threats! It associates the groveling courtier calling upon Canute to say to the sea, "thus far shall thy proud waves come but no farther." The omnipotent people, when they will it, can put up and pull down presidents, institutions, and governments. All are of their creation, and live and move by their sufferance, and obey their behests, when they are true to themselves. The government officials are their servants, not their masters. Such is the theory and the condition of practical constitutional liberty. The work of restoration and reconstruction can only be performed by the great agency of a National Convention. It is equally necessary for the North and the South. It must clear away the vast mass of debris and rubbish that the rebels, and the destructives, who hold power, have heaped upon our entire system, and reconstruct and restore the Federal Constitution and laws of Congress, and the State constitutions and laws, the entire Government and the Union as they were. If the people prove unequal to this work their destiny is certain; it is a military despotism and a master.

[NOTE.—The portion of this speech between the point where Senator Wilson called me to order and here, was cut off by his question of order being sustained. He had been permitted to pour out upon me falsehood and scurrility in three long speeches without interruption. G. D.]

38

After being called to order by Senator WILSON, and the question of order being sustained by the Senate, Mr. DAVIS resumed:

Mr. President, I will forego the further personal notice which I had intended to take of the Senator from Massachusetts. I felt that I had an account to settle with him, and it was my purpose to have a full settlement; but I acquiesce in the judgment of the Senate, and I will now proceed to the legitimate conclusion of my speech, the terms of which I suppose will be literally in order. Before which I will set the Senator from Wisconsin [Mr. DOOLITTLE] right on a few points of fact. The Senator from Massachusetts opened the debate on the resolution for my expulsion in a written speech, full of personal invectives and coarse abuse. I replied at length, but made no other speech. The Senator immediately rejoined, yet more offensively. Some days afterward the Senator withdrew his resolution, but, before doing so, made another speech fraught with gross personalities. I had prepared a summary from the Senator's speeches of his many attacks upon me personally, and intended to square the account. The Senate have cut me off from that privilege, and I think have done me injustice; but I must submit to its judgment, and will conclude my remarks.

Mr. President, the people of Massachusetts, as a whole, have always been strongly marked. Intellectual, energetic, active, latently brave, arrogant, conceited, inquisitive, meddlesome, not satisfied to manage their own business but ever trying to take charge of other people's, communicative yet secretive, alert, inventive, covetous, selfish, practical in business, ideal in doctrine, rational and skeptical in religion, with a moral sense consisting rather of habit than sentiment, swaying from one extreme opinion to another, and in all dogmatical, intolerant, fanatical, persecuting, and cruel; and yet her people cherish and hug to their bosom all their peculiarities, though many of them are revolting deformities.

It is seen from this sketch that her characteristics are strikingly and extensively mixed, giving efficiency at the same time for great mischief and great good. Yet no State of the Union, and few communities of her numbers in any age, have produced a larger aggregate of mind or more numerous or higher specimens of individual men. At the era of the Revolution she gave, not only to the colonies but to mankind, Franklin, the Adamses Hancock, Quincy, Warren, Prescott, and Copley; in the succeeding generation, King, John Quincy Adams, Story, and Parsons, Whittimore, Whitney, Bowditch; and at a later day, Everett, Davis, Choate, Winthrop, and Cushing, Shaw, Parker, and the Curtises, Hilliard, Hillard, and Thomas, Prescott, Bancroft, and Motley, Longfellow and Bryant, Perkins and Healy, Morse, Story the sculptor, and Morton, and a host of others who have shed unfading luster not only upon their own names but upon America. High above all of them, that product of New Hampshire, and development of Massachusetts, is the intellectual giant, Daniel Webster, who, as a constitutional lawyer, Senator, and Secretary, is without a peer. In Plato, Bacon, Burke, and Webster, man made his grandest development of pure intellect; while oratory and statesmanship have had their highest illustrations in Demosthenes, Cicero, Chatham, and Clay.

Massachusetts has had one unadulterated heroic age, commencing with the dawn of the troubles of the colonies with the mother country and coming down to the adoption of the Federal Constitution. During that eventful period there is no stain upon her escutcheon. She was about to act a first and principal part with the other colonies in a great political drama, involving not only the destiny of them all, and of a continent, but which was to influence materially the woof and color of the world's after-history. In mind, enlarged views, and wise statesmanship; in a just and true appreciation of her rights and duties, and those of the other colonies; in courage, fortitude, wisdom, disinterestedness, and moral principle, she was up to the great occasion. She was in singleness possessed of and inspired by true, noble, unselfish, and patriotic purposes, and throughout all the perils and trials of that momentous time Massachusetts showed no weakness, but always strength and greatness. She made no mistakes, she committed no crimes, no excesses. Her people had the good sense to call for the counsel and guidance of her wise, virtuous, and great men, and the fruits were for the colonies nationality and independence, and for herself one of the purest and brightest chapters in history.

The shock of England's oppressive policy for the colonies first struck Massachusetts. She at once invoked the aid of the southern colonies, and it was rendered not only without hesitation, but with heartiness for a common cause. They knew that one fate awaited them all. In the imperishable language of Mr. Webster, "Shoulder to shoulder they went through the Revolution, hand to hand they stood around the Administration of Washington, and felt his own great arm lean on them for support." Purified by the bloody ordeal of the long war, and instructed by the inefficiency of the Articles of Confederation in peace, the Constitution was the product of all the lessons of their experience, of their concessions, and of their harmonized counsels. It was the consummation of all their work, the perfection of man's statesmanship. If it were possible for the people of the United States to uphold, to guard, and defend it in the same spirit in which it was formed it would be perpetual; the degree of its security will always be proportioned to the prevalence of that spirit.

But after a time Massachusetts swung away from the great political principles and ends to which she had so steadily adhered for more than a generation. She has since been working with all her characteristic activity, energy, and audacity for the overthrow of that wonderful fabric of government in the building up of which she bore so conspicuous a part. She has kept up an incessant attack upon all its compromises except those which redound to her own advantage. She has repudiated all her able and enlightened national men, with their broad and statesmanlike views of Constitution, laws, and policy; she has surrendered to sectionalists, radicals, and factionists, to knaves and demagogues, to factitious philanthropists and clerical politicians and hypocrites, to men of one idea, and fatally bent on carrying that out, though Constitution and liberty thereby perish, to mannikins in intellect and soul, who are wholly incapable of her wise and good government, or any just appreciation of her relations, duties, and obligations both to the United States and the other States. She has permitted men, who can ruin but not rule, to make her one of the principal architects of the great national ills that are upon us.

She once garnel for herself and the whole country a great crop of imperishable glory; but she is now working as efficiently as the southern rebels for its degradation and ruin. When she shall have returned to her old political moorings, to the principles and spirit that ruled her when the foundations of our government were laid, and shall have thrown from herself the perverted and deformed dwarfs that now beset her like a legion of horrible incubuses, and have called back into her service her able, patriotic, and virtuous statesmen, the work of reunion and reconstruction will be speedily consummated. For that mighty work then, indeed, would Massachusetts be potential.

www.ingramcontent.com/pod-product-compliance
Lightning Source LLC
Chambersburg PA
CBHW021603270326
41931CB00009B/1357